States of Equilibrium

John Burton EdD

Crown House Publishing

www.crownhouse.co.uk

First published by

Crown House Publishing Ltd
Crown Buildings, Bancyfelin, Carmarthen, Wales, SA33 5ND, UK
www.crownhouse.co.uk

and

Crown House Publishing Ltd
P.O.Box 223, Williston, VT 05495-2223, USA
www.CHPUS.com

www.crownhouse.co.uk

British Library of Cataloguing-in-Publication Data
A catalogue entry for this book is available
from the British Library.

ISBN 1899836896

LCCN 2002116717

Printed and bound in the UK by
The Cromwell Press
Trowbridge
Wiltshire

*To my parents for countless contributions in so
many forms.*

Table of Contents

List of Figures

List of Tables

Acknowledgements

I would like to express appreciation to the fine folk at Crown House Publishing for their patience and persistence in working with me over the course of producing this book. I would also like to thank Bob Bodenhamer and Michael Hall for their gracious willingness to assist me with fine-tuning this work. They made invaluable contributions. I also want to thank my wife Kris for her unwavering support and encouragement throughout this project. Finally, I want to express appreciation for the one who makes all things possible. I remain in awe and appreciation.

Preface

This book represents a step toward a deeper understanding of the human personality and how to attain higher levels of human development. The theory presented here is called the "equilibrium theory" and incorporates concepts from other models to create a hybrid theory of personality and human development. The basis of this equilibrium theory comes from original work by Clark Hull (1947) and Walter Cannon (1932). Clark Hull developed what came to be known as "drive theory". The drive theory was originally based on our physiological systems, and maintains that as humans we are driven to achieve and maintain physiological balance. Cannon referred to this drive as homeostasis-the characteristic of maintaining a steady internal physiological state in spite of environmental changes. For example, the need to satisfy hunger and thirst seeks to restore and maintain blood sugar and hydration equilibrium in our bodies.

In the theory presented here, I have applied the drive theory, or Cannon's homeostasis, to our states of emotion. While we may temporarily lose emotional balance, we seek to return to it in spite of environmental changes. The dynamics of our emotional states draws on the work of Michael Hall (1995, 2000), who developed the concept of Meta-States[R]. I draw heavily from this concept and his work with emotional states. I believe we are driven to achieve and maintain equilibrium in emotions. Emotions exist on a continuum. Any single emotional state exists in a range of say, 1 to 9, and, in general, the larger collection of emotional states exists along a continuum of intensity. We operate best by remaining within a reasonable midrange of emotions, neither too high nor too low.

This is not to say we do not or should not experience intense emotions. We do experience such emotions and they are appropriate and useful at times. The point is that, after we experience these extremes of emotion, we are *driven* to return to equilibrium. Otherwise, we restrict ourselves to emotional extremes. Remaining at an emotional extreme limits our resourcefulness in responding to situations in daily life. But equilibrium theory is not just about practicality of emotional states. We seem to possess an innate need to return to and operate from these moderate emotional states as our natural resting level. When we believe these balanced emotional states are blocked from us, we develop psychological symptoms. By functioning from an extreme of emotion and not returning to equilibrium, we experience classic psychological symptoms such as anxiety and depression.

This drive for equilibrium has several influential variables that affect our ability to maintain this state. The two most influential factors in allowing or impeding equilibrium are the levels of human development and our cognitive style of processing information. A third significant variable is the events that occur during our life and how the first two variables act as filters to give powerful meaning to the events. We then apply these beliefs to allow or block our innate drive for equilibrium. In our childhood, we form fundamental beliefs about self, life, and others. In the process of forming these beliefs, we also determine which emotional states are safe and which are dangerous to us. This relationship with our states determines whether and how we can let our self shift from and regain equilibrium.

These early beliefs make up our original maps of the world, but our ability to make these maps is most limited during our childhood. During our earliest years we operate from the most primitive levels of human development. Our reasoning power is also limited, owing to our early cognitive ability. This limited human development, combined with limited reasoning ability of our childhood, plays a significant role in how we move through the range of emotions.

I'll use a short analogy to explain the concept of equilibrium as it applies to our emotional states. It uses the game of tennis to represent the concept of states and equilibrium. Once the ball is in play after the serve, a tennis player will generally position himself at the center of the court, somewhere near the back line. He does this to get the best view of the incoming returned ball *and* the center position allows him the best range of motion to either side. If his opponent hits the ball to one side of the court, the player can run over to it and hit the ball back. But what does the player do immediately after hitting the ball back? He returns to center. Positioning himself at center keeps him in the best position to reach and return any ball hit to his court.

This center position equates to equilibrium. We naturally gravitate there because it grants us the most flexibility and range. We can use a variety of states away from equilibrium to respond to changes in our environment, but we always seek to return to center. Limiting ourselves to *dis*equilibrium—off-center states—limits our effectiveness in life.

In this analogy, disequilibrium, or dysfunction, occurs because of bad experiences at the center position, motivating a shift for survival. Imagine a child just learning the game of tennis. She gets positioned by her teacher at just the right place on the court, back and center. This is all new to the girl. She has no point of reference.

Shortly after her first few successful returns, she sees a ball hit right at her. She can't get out of the way and it's not going to miss her body. *Plunk!* The little girl takes one right in the stomach before she could deflect it. "Ouch!" that hurt. Now she's a bit skittish waiting for the next ball to come over the net. Remembering what just happened, she's not so sure she wants to stand where she had been, right in the middle. Maybe if she moves just a bit over to one side she'll be safer. Well, the next ball that comes over the net is just as hard and hits her in the shin. Now the damage mounts and she is cautious of standing in the center or even close to it. She does not know how to defend herself adequately. She now begins to form beliefs about this "game" called tennis: it's dangerous and you can get hurt if you stand in the wrong place.

The child positions herself several steps to one side of center for the next exchange. She braces herself with fear of what's upcoming. The next ball that comes over the net is much softer and off to the far side. She tries hard and runs as fast as she can to get there, but she can't reach the ball. If she'd been at the center of the court she could have reached it for sure. She had formed beliefs about the game—dangerous!—and now she begins to form beliefs about herself. She thinks she's not competent because she could not get to the ball. But the real problem came from her initial belief that the game is dangerous because she must stand at the center. In order to feel safe she moved off to one side.

This analogy describes the essence of the concept of equilibrium and the process and consequences of disequilibrium. We naturally gravitate to equilibrium states, not just because they serve us better but because we feel "centered" or whole and we are driven to experience this. If emotionally painful events happen during our childhood while we occupy states of equilibrium, or any states for that matter, we abandon these states as a survival mechanism. We then operate from a position of emotional imbalance while longing for our lost equilibrium.

As you read through this book you will see references to the work of Jung, Skinner, Maslow and Rogers, Erikson and Loevinger, to name a few. These foundational theories of human nature combine nicely to explain the theory of equilibrium. Essentially, our personality stems from the relationship we have with our states of emotion. This relationship stems from our cognitive and developmental frames of reference for experiencing the world. Overriding this collection of dynamics is the inevitable force of the drive for equilibrium. This book is about what happens along the way as we navigate a course to achieve what we must: emotional equilibrium.

Introduction

The Nature of Equilibrium

The dark gray cloud with hues of blue, green and yellow extends in a funnel to the ground, forming a tornado. The spiraling clouds and accompanying torrents of rain within a hurricane move across the ocean onto land, drenching the countryside.

What do these and other acts of nature have in common? They each illustrate nature's innate drive for equilibrium. The tornado funnel provides a pathway for heavier cold air to travel down and take its proper place below while the lighter warm air that was trapped beneath spirals upward. One theory about hurricanes holds that these storms take water from a source where it is plentiful and move it to a location where it is in short supply, restoring greater balance.

In these cases and throughout nature, forces work to create and sustain equilibrium. And since humans are part of nature, we also strive to achieve and maintain equilibrium. This book presents a theory of human personality, that we are driven to achieve and maintain emotional equilibrium.

Equilibrium, as the concept is used here, refers to states of mind at a balance point on a continuum rather than states at an extreme. Equilibrium states include those such as assertiveness rather than the extremes of passivity or aggression. Another example of equilibrium is the state of care versus obsession or indifference. "Interdependent" represents equilibrium on another continuum while "very dependent" and "very independent" represent a loss of equilibrium. Equilibrium is also achieved when a person acts as an ambivert, socially flexible. The person who acts as a pure introvert or extrovert does not reach this balance point. Many states of mind exist within each of us. The states that occupy the midrange on a continuum I refer to as states of equilibrium. Equilibrium states allow flexibility, foresight and patience, which in turn allow a more effective response.

But, more than just existing and generally being more effective, we have a compelling attraction to these states of equilibrium. They are a sort of psychological gravity. Though we may draw on and use states outside the equilibrium range, we are driven to return to center. We start our life free to utilize these balanced states and strive to keep using them. If we experience emotional pain while in a state of equilibrium we shift away from this state to survive the emotional pain associated with the state. All the while our unconscious, instinctive drive is to return to living from these states. How do we come to leave the balanced states and can we overcome the restrictions?

The central concept in this book is that the human personality is organized around achieving states of equilibrium. This drive for balance has been known for some time as it applies to our physiological states, such as body temperature, blood sugar, and heart rate (Cofer and Appley, 1964). The drive theory was originally used to describe the process of our natural drive for physiological equilibrium. I believe this drive for equilibrium can also rightly be applied to our mental states, providing new understandings about how our personality develops and operates. We will also find how personality can evolve by choice to restore equilibrium. In this book I will identify and describe the factors that influence our drive for equilibrium. Four factors combine to determine whether we do or do not function from equilibrium:

1. The existence of mental states within us—we each possess a wide variety of states of mind that operate with certain predictable dynamics;
2. Accessing and utilizing any given state of mind-our willingness to access these equilibrium states freely;
3. Our level of human development;
4. Our cognitive style of processing sensory information.

The concept of mental state will be used very often through this book. By "state" I mean a particular mental or emotional condition such as confusion, curiosity, frustration, relief, or joy. Hundreds of states exist. Each state contains perception, beliefs, emotions, and behavioral responses. We perceive, think, feel, and act one way from a state of discouragement, while very different contents make up the state of joy. States may have a common name we all use, such as discouragement or joy, but the way the state is represented in each person is unique. States also play a crucial role in one's personality. After all, these states of mind make up our personality. We may be seen as outgoing, shy, aloof or a leader. These states, or whichever ones we display most often, come to be known as our personality.

States exist in three general forms: primary states, Meta-States[R] (Hall, 1995, 2000), and gestalt states. Primary states are states of being about an event we directly experience or observe. They include anger, fear, sadness, and joy. Hundreds of primary states exist. A person may feel angry when his friend stands him up for a lunch date. On the other hand he may feel curious, relieved, or even worried by the snub. The state chosen depends greatly on how the person perceives the event. In general, primary states refer to some external event but do include physical sensations.

Meta-States[R] are states of mind about another state of mind within us. Meta-States[R] are how we feel about our feelings or what we think about our thoughts. After first feeling angry over his friend's standing him up, he may then move to feeling guilty about his anger. In this case, guilt serves as a meta-state. Any state can exist as either a primary state or meta-state. The difference is whether the state is about an event (primary) or about another state of consciousness within the person (meta).

Meta-States[R] can continue nearly infinitely—the process is known as *reflexive thinking*. A person could feel angry and then guilty about his anger. He could then take the meta-state process a step further and feel disgusted about feeling guilty about his initial anger. Maybe he believes he has good reason to be angry about his friend's behavior. After all, this friend stood him up the last two times they'd arranged to meet for lunch. This thinking may lead to a meta-state of feeling justified about his initial anger. The key point is that this layering of meta-states can go on almost endlessly.

Gestalt states represent the third type of state and refer to a sort of super state that consists of several other states. Gestalt states very often turn up in the process of helping clients reach a more effective state. For example, when one is working with a client to help her to ascend her meta-states, she may step into a state she calls "euphoria". Now, for her, this state may consist of several other states such as confidence, calmness, happiness, and strength. You can identify a gestalt state by asking the person to name the state she finds when she combines the previously named states of confidence, calmness, happiness, and strength.

Gestalt states exist in resourceful styles but also as severely limiting types. A person who despises himself may be operating from a gestalt state of despising himself. This state may be made up of other states that include disgust, irritation, incompetence, and several others.

States of mind, primary and meta, operate by certain principles. The first, as we have just illustrated, is that meta-states can go on indefinitely in layers. The second principle is that we each choose, consciously or unconsciously, our own states to experience in life. Third, each meta-state serves to override and dominate any states beneath them. Each time we experience a state of mind and then go out of it to associate into another, the second state will modify or change the original state. The highest meta-state into which the person associates serves as the state from which the person thinks, feels, and behaves. As Gregory Bateson put it (1972), higher states of consciousness always moderate those states beneath them.

We each choose our own states to experience in life.

But how do we end up with the states that we utilize, be they primary or meta-states? Theories of human ego development and cognitive development provide a way of understanding various age-related influences on using or avoiding these states of equilibrium. Developmental levels and cognitive processes act as filters, giving meaning to any life experience, even if the meaning and resulting state limits the person.

When we combine ego-development theories and cognitive development theories and their interaction with our states, a new model of human personality emerges. This model suggests that a person's state utilization determines personality and overall mental health. While we always strive for equilibrium, the states we utilize are determined by which states we perceive as being safe or unsafe to utilize. Of more significance toward mental health is that a person can overcome an aversion to any given state, choosing states that allow the most resourceful response to any given situation, the ultimate equilibrium.

Chapter One
Learning States

"Experience without emotion is void of learning."
—*Francis Bacon, English lawyer, philosopher and essayist.*

This simple, profound statement has remained with me since I read it more than 25 years ago. Bacon identified the element present in all learning over the course of our lives, which is that all learning is dependent upon emotional states. As used here, learning means a relatively enduring change in thinking or behavior that is due to experience. We associate into some emotional state in order to learn. It could also be said that all learning takes place in a trance, because when a person associates into a particular emotional state he goes into a light trance. A trance, as the term is used here, is a state of mind in which a person focuses on a single stimulus or a like group of stimuli to the exclusion of all others. To experience the principle of a trance state's presence in learning, what general state do you go into as you remember the first time you drove a car? While searching through your past experiences you go into your library of trances, don't you?

Each state of mind is exclusive to other states and has its own thoughts, emotions and behavioral tendencies.

Each trance state is made up of one or more states of mind. Each state of mind is exclusive and has its own thoughts, emotions, and behavioral tendencies. While a trance can be made up of several states, the crucial principle is that a trance sets boundaries, which will exclude some states and include others. When you focus on stimuli in certain ways you generate particular states of mind.

As an example, think about the state of optimism. To experience optimism fully, you must exclude pessimism. Optimism and pessimism are complex states that rely on the state of care as their foundation. Recognize that you have to care about an out-

1

explore two contrasting states. How do you feel Physically when experiencing both?

come to bother generating optimism or pessimism. In order to be optimistic, we must focus on part of a whole collection of stimuli, highlighting those parts that present a desired outcome.

Mind

Body / Physical Sensations

This trance state of optimism will then lead to various states of mind, such as eagerness, enthusiasm, joy, or exhilaration. Every state of mind also generates a "state of body"—we experience these as physical sensations. How do you feel physically when experiencing joy? How do you feel physically when you experience disappointment? How do they differ? With joy you may feel an energized lightness. With disappointment you will most likely experience lethargy and heaviness.

Our interaction with our states comes in one of two forms: we either associate into or dissociate from a state.

Our interaction with states of mind comes in two forms. We either experience the state (associated) or think about the state (dissociated). Fully engaging a particular state of mind is referred to as being *associated* into a state, having a direct, first-hand experience of it.

Being dissociated from a state means the person has awareness of a state and its attributes while not directly experiencing it. The dissociated perspective is the analytical point of view. For example, we are associated into the clothes we are presently wearing but dissociated from the ones hanging in our closet. Metaphorically, our unconscious mind contains all the clothes we've ever worn, and, in some theories, all the clothes that ever existed and have yet to exist.

Allow yourself to picture a recently pleasant event. When you see the mental picture, notice whether you see yourself in the picture or not. If you do not see yourself this means you are associated into the picture and state of mind that comes with the scene. If you do see yourself in the mental picture, this means you are in the dissociated position. Now, if you saw yourself in the picture, pop into yourself and experience the scene in a first-hand, associated way. If you did not see yourself in the first picturing of the scene, pop out of yourself so you now see yourself in the scene. Notice how the feelings associated with the two positions differ.

When we are associated, the feelings are more intense. When we are dissociated, the feelings are somewhat diminished.

The word "meta" means about, above, or beyond.

States exist in two forms, primary and meta. The word "meta" literally means about, above, or beyond. When we go to a position that is meta, we step out of the primary state, dissociate from it, rise above it and step into a state of mind that represents how we feel about the initial state. This process is beneficial if the primary state limits us, which is the case with most primary states. A limiting state is one that prevents a more resourceful response. Going meta allows the choice of a new state. Hopefully, we choose a more resourceful state. The meta-state always subsumes the one below and becomes the dominant state (Bateson, 1972). Virginia Satir (1983) identified the innate mental structure of meta-levels, while working on patterns of communication.

Michael Hall (1995, 2000) found that we can associate into multiple states by going to a meta-position invoking a state that incorporates several states. For example, imagine you have just received a job offer from the company that you really wanted to join. You may experience several states at the same time such as excitement, thrill, and honor. These three states form a gestalt that may be the meta-state you call euphoria.

Meta-States^R represent a gestalt of several states, which in turn creates a sort of superstate. This superstate presides over all states it subsumes.

Meta-States^R represent a gestalt of several states, which in turn creates a sort of superstate. This superstate presides over all states it subsumes. A meta-state is just a single state on a ladder of states with each successive state reaching a higher degree of consciousness. We can think about our thoughts and then think about the thoughts about our thoughts. We can repeat the meta-state process until we reach a place of pure potentiality, that conceptual place beyond words (Korzybski, 1933, 1994). This *can* be experienced, yet neither words nor symbols exist to describe the experience. Have you ever reached a place in your mind where you have said to a friend, "There are just no words to describe this feeling"? If you have, then you know about this state of mind. All internal resources exist within this pure-potentiality level of consciousness. They remain in storage for future use. All designs and ideas past and present are found in the place of pure potentiality.

In some ways it resembles the transcendent states described in Hindu and Buddhist traditions as nirvana or *samadhi*. It contains everything and yet is not any one thing. It is the place of genius. No limitations or boundaries exist here and all things are possible. Here, solutions exist for all issues. Ego disappears, because it does not fit and is not needed. We also lose personal need. There is no defensiveness, there are no deficiencies; all is present. We select from that state whatever suits the situation.

Consider any one leaf on a tree as representing a primary state. The leaf represents the state that interacts with the environment. Now consider the twig from which the leaf extends as a meta-state. Tracing this twig to its origin, we find a branch. The branch may connect to a larger branch that meets the trunk of the whole tree. Like meta-states, the twig affects the leaf, the branch affects the twig and the trunk affects the branch while the root system affects all parts. Moving beyond this is increasingly abstract. The individual tree is only one within a category of like trees. The broader category of all trees takes in the smaller group of like trees.

We can then extend this process to include all plant life, then, as our awareness expands, reach the point of all living things. Moving beyond this, we find the category of all things existing. Progressing further still, we arrive at the place of all that ever existed, is now existing, and is yet to exist. Beyond this we go to the place where all things exist in a state before any definition. They reside in a raw form, yet to be shaped, applied or even labeled. No words suffice for the all-inclusive contents. This is the place of pure potentiality.

Learning involves four basic steps: attending, encoding, storage, and retrieval.

This is also the process for acquiring information and accessing memory (Weiten, 1989). We could not learn anything without our memory.

Attending is simply the narrowing of your focus to a small range of items or information in your environment. The trance begins here. We bring in the information in our narrow focus through one or more of our senses. Initially, information processing takes place at the point of entry (sense organ). Complex processing and meaning-making then occur in our thalamus and various regions of our cerebral cortex.

Encoding happens when the brain establishes visual and/or verbal icons that represent the content of the material processed. These icons serve as file headings. By using a verbal or visual icon to represent the whole file contents we can store massive amounts of information. A picture becomes worth a thousand words or more. However, each of us is unique in how we represent the information we store. No two people create identical pictures even for the same information. So a word is also worth a thousand pictures.

Storage and **retrieval** rely on cues from the environment. If we interpret a situation as calling for an aggressive response, then we open the file marked "aggressive" and the corresponding responses emerge.

The meaning-making process first involves comparing new stimuli to previous learning rather than automatically creating new learning or categories of information.

Choosing the file that fits the situation depends on accurately assessing the environmental cues. The assessment depends partly on what environmental stimuli the person attends. It also depends on what meaning is attributed to the stimuli by the observer. This meaning-making process first involves comparing new stimuli to previous learning rather than automatically creating new learning or categories of information. If the current stimuli do not match a pre-existing file, then a new file or category of information gets created and stored in the brain.

Sometimes we misinterpret the cues in the environment and choose a response file that is not appropriate for the situation. When we misunderstand someone, for example, taking a comment out of context we may end up responding ineffectively. What one person calls aggressive another may have placed in the passive file. And so it remains, the map is not the territory. As Korzybski (1933, 1994) stated, we make maps or representations in our mind of the external world. But these maps become subjected to our limited awareness and misinterpretations of the external world. The result is that our internal map inaccurately represents the external world to some degree.

The idea that previous learning determines current responses relates to B. F. Skinner's (1974) learning theory. Skinner says we are a collection of response tendencies with various stimuli dictating to us. People respond to familiar cues in the environment in repetitive ways depending on their reinforcement history, their conditioning. I wonder if history repeats itself because people look to the past to decide how to respond in the present. If a current situation resembles an old situation, then the person just responds out of habit.

What would happen if we looked into our desired future to decide how to respond to our present? This This would result in a person's being outcome-oriented.

What would happen if we looked into our desired future to decide how to respond to our present? This would result in a person's being outcome-oriented. When a person plans his future, this plan usually works out best by working from a clearly formed future outcome. A well-formed outcome naturally prescribes states and behaviors consistent with its successful completion.

An example involving assertiveness shows how time-orientation can influence response choice. This is a story about a girl, Regina, raised by an overbearing and controlling mother. For Regina, being assertive seemed impossible, lest she run the risk of receiving her mother's severe punishment. As a result she believed being assertive was unsafe. To remain in a state of safety, Regina moved through the world in a passive manner. She did not voice differences of opinion or stand up for herself.

In one particular class, Regina needed to achieve an "A" in order to go on to graduate school. The course was very tough. She studied very hard and put in many hours of study for the exam, but she finished six points short of qualifying for graduate school. She decided to check over her final exam and found that the professor made a mistake in grading her test. Correcting the mistake would give her more than enough points to get into graduate school.

Regina then found herself faced with the dilemma of voicing or not voicing her opinion. She realized that taking this issue to her professor might lead to conflict. Her mind replayed her past experiences when she took up differences with her mother and got squelched. She became anxious and believed the only way to relieve the anxiety was to remain quiet and not say anything to her professor.

If Regina searched only her previous learning and memory files about how to express differences of opinion, she would have quietly accepted failing to make graduate school. However, looking into her future, she realized the person she wanted to be, and how she wanted her life to become. As a result of looking into her future for the resolution to the present, she voiced her position and received the grade change. This changed the course of her future, leading to a different outcome.

When you think about what you used to know, compared with what you know now, what new knowledge do you now have? And when you think about what you do not yet know and look into your future, knowing then what you want to know now, what do you now know and how will you use it?

Learning consequences

We now have an idea about what states of mind are and some of their properties. We also have an idea about the process of sensing information and how this information is then placed in our memory and recalled. I suggest that when it comes to the initial sensing of information that we sort all experiences into one of three categories:

1. Experiences that sustain or increase our wellbeing;
2. Experiences that threaten our safety or the continuation of our wellbeing;
3. Experiences that are neutral on the threat-safety scale.

The neutral experiences in the third category are of no interest and we quickly dismiss them as irrelevant. Since there is no vested interest, no learning occurs. We call these experiences boring, because not enough trance gets generated to foster learning.

This three-category sorting process makes up our first step in the learning process. We subject each experience we encounter to one of these three steps, making up our first line of defense or self-preservation. This process likely takes place in the unconscious mind and functions in an automatic sort of way. The process involves quickly comparing every single experience to a global criterion as to how it relates to self-preservation.

In order to determine the significance of the information sensed in the environment, we first think about our own existence. We bring this external information inside ourselves, and search for its relevance in maintaining our existence. This internal search is the trance state that takes place in learning. The process occurs regardless of the state from which we perceive. Simply put, we learn and remember what is most important to us. What is most important to us is, first, what keeps us alive and, second, what helps us evolve.

> **This internal search is the trance state that takes place in learning. The process occurs regardless of the state from which we perceive.**

We naturally pay more attention to information that we believe helps maintain our existence. Research indicates that epinephrine (a stimulant) secreted by the brain acts to enhance memory ability (McGaugh *et al.*, 1983). It provides energy for attending information. In a general sense, we notice an event, decide whether it is personally significant, and then respond by processing the information.

Emotions at this point seem rather reflexive, resembling Thorndike's[1] (Clifford, 1984) learning concept and Pavlov's conditioning. Any event (stimulus) that is personally important to us generates a chemical response within the individual, and this response also generates an emotion. An event is associated with triggering an emotion. But emotions are more than the result of a simple association process. No predetermined emotion is linked with any particular event.

Any event that is personally important to us generates a chemical response within the individual.

Several factors influence any emotion that results from experiencing an event. Any given association results from the individual's cognitive-perceptual style and his developmental level of functioning. At lower levels of human development we endow the environment with the power to determine emotions. At higher levels of development we become aware that we can choose our states of emotion.

The process of going from noticing a stimulus to experiencing an emotion happens so fast that it is easy to attribute the emotion to the external stimulus. As a result, we tend to avoid situations with characteristics similar to originally distressing events. Our purpose is to prevent re-experiencing unpleasant states. It seems that phobias originate in this way. A person may appear to have a fear of water and so avoid being in water, but this person really avoids water to avoid the state he *associates* with water: fear and its many forms.

At lower levels of human development we endow the environment with the power to determine our emotions. At higher levels of development we becomes aware that we can choose our states of emotion.

Thinking that events cause emotional states doesn't stop at phobias. Why wouldn't this same mechanism of believing a state is caused by an event be a factor in any learning, be it resourceful or limiting about states? I believe that early in life we enter into a

---

[1]The Psychologist, Edward Thorndike, identified three laws of learning. One, known as the law of effect, states that when a choice meets with a satisfying outcome, the same choice will likely be repeated. Equilibrium theory would say that when a chosen state meets with a satisfying outcome, that state is likely to be chosen again for a similar situation.

relationship with our states and judge them as either pleasant or unpleasant, safe or unsafe, depending on the event we experience while associated into a state. The way we experience the event and consequent belief about the state is a function of our level of cognitive and human development. We then proceed to work toward or away from these various states according to the value we have attached to them.

For example, we do not just move toward success or away from failure. Rather, we move toward or away from the states of mind that we *associate* with success or failure. As an example of the supposed away-from-failure strategy, let us look at the case of a woman who wants to put in many hours of overtime at work. She believes this will lead to promotion and a raise, along with some power and status. But these benefits serve only to move her away from her bad memory of growing up in a very poor family and feeling inferior to others. With the success, she believes she can end up experiencing a sense of high self-worth. The behavior of putting in overtime in order to gain position, money, and power is really just designed to leave the state of inferiority behind in exchange for a state of high self-worth.

The problem with an "away-from" strategy is that, unless the original state of inferiority is removed, she can never fully experience her sense of high self-worth. The earlier sense of inferiority will act as a hole in her self-worth, allowing the good feeling to leak out. The result is a nearly constant need to replenish.

The belief that an event determines a state is the dynamic behind addictions. The addiction is believed to be about the behavior or substance. But the addiction is actually an addiction to the emotional state that follows the behavior.

Addiction is actually an addiction to the emotional state that follows the behavior.

This learning process of associating events with states is not necessarily bad or good. By activating resources and properly responding to relevant stimuli, we effectively use our survival mechanisms. Emotions of any sort intensify our awareness and stimulate memory-enhancing hormones, increasing our ability to process information and adjust to the situation at hand. This in turn promotes survival. The trick of course is accurately sizing up a situation and choosing an effective response. Personal distress, if experienced, stems from the emotion we associate with any of these learning experiences.

Personal distress, if experienced, stems from the emotion we associate with any of these learning experiences.

An example may help in understanding how we limit ourselves by associating certain states with events. I once worked with a client, Marnie, who could not allow herself to feel good about her accomplishments. She had experiences in her past that led her to stop herself from feeling good about any of her many professional accomplishments. Marnie could let herself feel good only if she felt bad about the good feeling.

In counseling, I pointed out how she could feel good about how well she did at feeling bad about feeling good. This move prompted the first step in eventually removing the middle layer, the bad feeling. As we went up the "meta-state ladder", Marnie began recognizing (literally, generating new cognitions) how absurd her process was of alternating layers of good and bad feelings. This led to her balancing the two emotions, good and bad, through integrating them. Marnie found a happy medium that was neither too bad nor too good.

The process of effective adaptation

Beginning with the idea that stimuli are either threatening or self-preserving, we move to the next step in learning. Learning, or adapting to any situation, involves two general processes: assimilation and accommodation. Assimilating means taking in information, while accommodating means reconfiguring existing beliefs in response to the new information. The developmental theorist Jean Piaget (1965) identified these concepts and their role in the learning process. According to Piaget, intelligence is an individual's ability to cope with changing external conditions by continuously reorganizing her map of the world and responding accordingly, assimilating and accommodating.

Assimilating means taking in information while accommodating means reconfiguring existing beliefs in response to the new information.

The challenges to effective assimilating are deleting, distorting, and generalizing the information that we perceive (Bandler and Grinder, 1975). Once we take in the information, the next step is either adjusting the new to fit the old, or adjusting the old in accordance with the new. If all we do is assimilate without adjusting, we force-fit all new stimuli into our pre-existing beliefs (overgeneralizing), which means that, according to our perceptions, nothing new ever happens. But the only way to force-fit new ideas into the old mold is to ignore the exceptions or twist them so they become distorted.

When a friend of yours suddenly behaves "out of character" you perceive his behavior and assimilate it into what you already know about him. How does his uncharacteristic behavior relate to his previously established pattern, and what does this all mean now? Do you disregard, investigate, or simply adjust to the behavior? The belief you form in response to this aberrant behavior is known as *accommodating* and the response you choose to the situation is *adapting*.

The process of accommodating happens when new experiences lead to updated maps of the territory. Accommodation leads to new awareness and responses that take into account the changes in the environment. Ideally, we accommodate when we take in (assimilate) information that is inconsistent with existing beliefs. Children initially attempt to understand new experiences by applying old learning. If this does not work, the child changes her existing concept of the world for a more accurate picture of the situation and more effective solutions.

Accommodating is similar to what happens when a person chooses what state to use for a given situation.

While assimilating provides information about our environment, accommodating occurs when we choose the state we believe most likely to create our desired outcome. We repeat this cycle throughout our lifespan regardless of age. When a person assimilates and accommodates effectively, he can reach a state that Piaget (1965) termed "equilibrium".

There is also a stage between assimilating and accommodating that plays a crucial role. When a person first assimilates new information, he shifts to a position termed *disequilibrium*. Disequilibrium is experienced when current information and behavior no longer fit the new circumstance. Ideally, the person then accommodates, restoring equilibrium. For example, if you are driving on a dry road, you may drive fairly aggressively. But, when the rain begins to fall and your car skids a little on the wet road surface, you accommodate by recognizing the changed conditions. Now you slow down and drive more carefully. This is adaptation. This mismatch between behavior and situation motivates accommodating, driving more slowly.

Piaget stated that disequilibrium motivates learning because people strive for equilibrium. This same principle is believed to apply to states. While we may temporarily utilize an extreme state, we do so only for a purpose. Afterwards, we feel motivated to resume operating from equilibrium states. Assimilating without accommodating does not allow for a change in behavior or states of mind, even in the face of evidence that calls for a shift.

Piaget stated that disequilibrium motivates learning because people strive for equilibrium.

The inability to assimilate and accommodate effectively, for whatever reason, limits a person's adaptability and problem-solving ability. The overassimilating person operates from a highly egocentric position. Taken to an extreme, a person who only assimilates without accommodating verges on a delusional belief system. This is because the person who does not accommodate keeps a firm grip on his old belief system. He then chooses behavior from the old belief system rather than basing responses on the current situation. New information is force-fitted into the pre-existing belief system, isolating the person from the current reality. This person lives out the old saying, "Don't confuse me with the facts, I've already made up my mind."

The cause of this overassimilating likely comes from past experience. Feeling phobic about a particular resource state, for example, could make for this inflexibility. If a particular resource-ful state is emotionally uncomfortable, a person will not utilize it even though new information calls for an adjusted response. He may restrict himself to a narrow range of states because of past emotionally painful experiences with other states.

To illustrate the process of how a person gets to a point of res-tricting state utilization, let's use the metaphor of a man putting together a storage cabinet. While the upright and horizontal pieces fit together and hold each other up fairly well, additional support is needed if the cabinet is going to be fully useful. To increase the stability and strength, he uses flathead screws to hold the pieces in place. Naturally, he then needs a flathead screw-driver to finish securing the cabinet. But what if this man had been injured in the past while using a flathead screwdriver? The result could be that he has a fear of the screwdriver and no longer even keeps it in his toolbox.

To work around the fear he chooses another tool that he hopes will work, the next best substitute that he thinks will do the job. He tries a knife blade but can't tighten the screws enough to secure the cabinet. He uses his fingernails, a coin, and other makeshift tools that have a profile similar to the banned flathead screwdriver, but nothing works. The end result is that he can use the storage cabinet in only a limited way because it is not stable and secure.

In this metaphor, the screwdriver represents a mental state. When an emotionally painful event happens while associated into a particular state the person decides the state is off-limits because it is believed unsafe. From this point forward he refuses to assoc-iate into that dangerous state. The result is personal limitation, for which he then attempts to compensate. Rejecting a state and the compensating that follows results from misperceiving the properties of the rejected state. The state is believed to possess the ability to cause the trauma.

Although it may *look* as if the emotionally injured person were generalizing from the original traumatic situation, then avoiding any situations that are similar to it, the actual process is different. The person avoids states rather than situations. The external appearance is that of generalizing from situation to similar situation, but the motivation to avoid a situation comes from the belief that the situation "causes" the state

While a person believes a state is made dangerous by a situation, thus avoids the situation, the state used in the situation is what the person really fears.

Essentially, a phobic state exists about the avoided state, not about the situation. While a person believes a state is made dangerous by the situation, thus avoids the situation, the state used in the situation is what the person really fears. The external appearance is that of avoiding situations that the person fears but the truth is that the person fears the state that is triggered by the situation.

The dynamics of panic attacks with agoraphobia is a good example of avoiding circumstances that seem to cause the feared state. Here the person suffering from panic attacks starts avoiding any situation in which she's experienced a panic attack. She uses this strategy to avoid panic because she associates panic with certain settings. But the panic continues to happen in different settings. Her world gradually shrinks in an effort to avoid the broadening "causes" of her panic attacks.

Soon, the effort to prevent panic attacks leads to a generalized fear of being out in public. The result is a person who is almost homebound. In some severe cases of agoraphobia the person can actually reach a point of fearing calm. She was calm right before her panic came out of the blue. Now, when she feels calm she remembers the ensuing panic from the past.

A general principle applies to this process of avoiding states associated with upsetting events. The severity of a trauma while a person is associated into a particular state, compared to previous experiences in that state, determines how the person feels about utilizing the state in the future. One bad experience while associated into a particular state is not enough to offset a history of many good experiences with that state. But, if a person believes a state to be off-limits, he will then utilize the next closest approximation of the state.

15

If a person believes a state to be off-limits, he will then utilize the next closest approximation of the state.

If all hell breaks loose while a person is experiencing a state of calm, he may find that he is reluctant to allow himself to experience calm in the future. Discomfort with the state of calm often happens in children who are raised by alcohol-abusing parents. The child may actually feel anxious about feeling calm. This develops because, just when he starts to feel comfortable about feeling calm, one of his parents goes on a drinking binge and flies into an alcohol-fueled rage. Even when the atmosphere at home settles down, it provides no comfort.

The longer the home remains calm, the more his anxiety increases. He comes to believe that it's only a matter of time before the inevitable next drinking binge, and chaos explodes again. Calm is not enjoyed, only dreaded. It actually becomes easier to deal with the known enemy, chaos, than the time bomb that is calm. This person may actually unconsciously create chaos because it provides a familiar, relative safety.

If the trauma is severe enough or repeats enough, he may not allow himself to experience calm at all, even from a meta-state of anxiety. People can sometimes feel an "uneasy calm" by associating into anxiety and attempting to experience a dissociated state of calm. Follow the reasoning carefully in the next statement. He actually feels calmer by feeling anxious about feeling calm than by experiencing calm directly. And, if the trauma continues, then the uneasy calm will be abandoned in favor of a state that feels safer, such as feeling tense.

The paradox of trying to feel calm through various states of anxiety continues. This frustrating effort escalates if the traumatic experiences continue, moving the person further and further away from the state he craves, calm, and the equilibrium it brings. Depression then follows over the loss of the original state of calm. He believes he can no longer safely experience calm and so mourns its loss.

In a way, we limit ourselves and draw inaccurate conclusions by judging our compensating efforts.

In this way, we limit ourselves and draw inaccurate conclusions about ourselves by judging our compensation efforts. If we believe we are our states, identity statements spring out such as "I am always anxious" or "I can never ever feel calm". These statements are really just reflections of the person's relationships with his states. We are then tempted to make even more damaging identity conclusions. A sort of meta-identity can follow. If "I am always anxious" then maybe "I am an incompetent person". After all, how ineffective does always feeling anxious make a person?

People respond to their environment based on what is perceived in it, but this is only half of the story. The map is not the territory: it is a limited perception of the environment that leads to less than complete understanding. But we still attempt to make and use practical maps of the external world. These maps and their contents, our perceptions of the external world, powerfully influence our decisions.

The other half of the mapmaking story, and equally influential, is that we make maps of our internal world. Our internal map evaluates the safety or danger of our emotional states.

We rely on this map to decide which states we use and for which situations. This map is not the territory either. We may perceive states as unavailable when these states would actually provide paths to solutions. As an example, "I'm afraid to speak up in that situation" is a common expression of an internal roadblock. The person believes she cannot utilize a particular state, such as assertiveness, in a particular situation. Therapy overcomes the roadblocks and allows her resource-state utilization. Metaphorically speaking, she then finds the tool or state that really fits the job. The ability and willingness to adjust responses according to the situation is known as adaptation.

Chapter Two
Primitive Cognitive Tools and Early Belief Forming

The processes of assimilating and accommodating that lead to adaptation or equilibrium rely heavily on our perceptive and cognitive ability. This chapter describes the perceptual-cognitive processes that produce our limiting beliefs and awareness. (A limiting belief is essentially a negative belief about self, others, or life. Limiting beliefs are beliefs that a person forms in response to emotional trauma. These beliefs set unnecessary limits on a person's ability.)

This is a good moment to introduce a branch of psychology known as Neuro-Linguistic Programming (NLP) and combine some of its theory with findings of Jean Piaget. Discoveries from these branches of psychology yield the explanation of how we arrive at limited awareness and limiting beliefs, and how we can expand our awareness, leaving behind these former limitations.

Piaget identified some of the ways that children think and correlated these thinking patterns with the age of the child. Much disagreement exists within the cognitive-developmental field as to just when children exhibit the thinking patterns identified by Piaget, but there does seem to be general agreement about the thinking patterns themselves. (If you want to explore this further, Margaret Donaldson's *Children's Minds* (1979) is a good place to start.)

My purpose in presenting the work of Piaget is not to support or refute the different theories on when children think the way they do. Rather, I want to consider various thinking patterns children use, and their influence on human development.

The collection of tools and beliefs that comprise NLP continues evolving. From its inception as a distinct method of studying the human experience and creating personal change techniques, NLP continues to sharpen the understanding of human thinking, feeling, and behaving. NLP finds that our problems are misguided behavioral strategies that limit a person to narrow and rigid perceptions about the environment and self, resulting from poor assimilating.

These deficient perceptions limit beliefs, thoughts, feelings, and behaviors.

The solution to the perceptual error is simply the inverse of the strategy that led to the limitation. In other words, becoming aware of anything from a different category of information expands awareness, flexibility, and choice.

Change any one ingredient in the recipe and the result is a different product. With meta-stating we create a recipe that produces a delicious product.

In *Timeline Therapy™ and the Basis of Personality*, James and Woodsmall (1988) point out that *significant emotional events* (SEEs) are sufficient for generating limiting beliefs. A SEE is an experience that is an emotionally painful event, an emotional trauma. A SEE must vary from the norm of life either in intensity or frequency. This notion is part of the principles of basic learning theory. Hearst (1988) found that stimuli must be novel or especially intense to influence a person's behavioral choice.

Also of significance to this book's theory is the concept of stimulus contiguity, identified by Pavlov (1927). Stimulus contiguity occurs when a stimulus powerful enough to evoke a response is presented and *quickly* followed by any other stimulus. The second stimulus will acquire a similar power for evoking a response to first (Pavlov called it the *conditioned stimulus*).

Stimulus contiguity occurs when a stimulus powerful enough to evoke a response is presented and *quickly* followed by any other stimulus. The second stimulus will acquire the same power.

Pavlov's conditioning principle, combined with the phenomena of SEEs, forms the basis of the theory of states of equilibrium: a person's state at the time of a SEE becomes the conditioned stimulus. The person then perceives the state at the time of the SEE as dangerous to his welfare. The SEE naturally draws the person to make some sense of the event and explain how it happened. As a result of this thinking, limiting beliefs about self may be born. Certain states become off-limits for the person. He then compensates for the unavailable state by drawing on the next best state.

Imagine growing up in a family with members who never raise their voices. One day the girl in this family gets curious about something that she was told not to touch. The father suddenly bursts out and raises his voice in response to his daughter's behavior. His yelling is such an exceptional event, that it makes a very deep impression on the child.

The child was in a state of curiosity at the time of the traumatic event. Curiosity then becomes associated with the negative event. The next time she feels curious about something she may ask if she can take a look at it beforehand.

Not all consequences of SEEs are necessarily bad. SEEs can have some positive consequences by encouraging certain states to be off-limits. If a child receives strong punishment while in a state called "deceptive", he may never deceive again. While the child may feel that he was punished, the mind believes that the *state* was punished, so the "deceptive state" will not be used again.

For an event to qualify as a SEE, the event must stand out from the norm.

For an event to qualify as a SEE, the event must stand out from the norm, whatever the norm may be. In another family, the norm is frequent voice raising, so a loud protest does not stand out unless a voice rises beyond a certain threshold or involves some physical abuse. The physically abusive event becomes a SEE, altering a child's state and future use of the state.

A SEE that recurs over a period of time can set in motion a series of consequences. In adulthood, a person may never argue because disagreements remind him of his father's yelling. This person's coping strategies usually involve retreating from confrontation and passively hoping others will meet his needs, instead of assertively taking steps to satisfy his own needs in life. This person tends toward a passive-dependent style of behavior, easily giving in to others' requests to avoid potential conflict.

However, this same person could choose the other disequilibrium state. This state might consist of a pushy, argumentative style in response to the SEE, employing a sort of pre-emptive strike strategy. He also has a difficult time being still and letting the *status quo* remain in place, so he continues to impose his will on others, and this will often changes. He believes that if things do settle down then he just moves that much closer to the dangerous state of calm. Keeping things unsettled avoids the equilibrium states he associates with his father's temper outbursts.

These forceful, argumentative people sometimes believe they can prevent the "dangerous" state of peace or calm by keeping things in an uproar. People who use this strategy of imposing their will on others and keeping things unsettled I refer to as "takers." Their coping strategy usually involves proactive pursuit of their needs but through others. This "taker" person may tend toward aggressive and pressuring ways while the "asker" tends toward passive styles, relying on hopes that others will meet his needs. Neither the "asker" nor the "taker" reflects resolution of the emotional issues stemming from the SEE.

Sometimes during childhood a great many SEEs happen and become associated with a variety of states. If enough unresolved SEEs occur, numerous states become off-limits because of a large collection of limiting beliefs. These processes and decisions leading to limiting beliefs often take place in the unconscious mind. Once the limiting belief is in place, it continues operating from the unconscious mind. It just acts automatically without our conscious consent.

Some theories refer to this unconscious steering device as an "unconscious part". In this use, unconscious parts are automatic response states that limit us, restricting constructive response options. The process of developing many "unconscious parts" evokes the image of a Frankenstein's monster coming to life owing to several especially traumatic events in childhood. All of the "unconscious parts" are assembled into a "monster" that eventually runs amok.

Limiting beliefs eventually accumulate enough consequences from poor decisions and backfire, causing more emotional distress. These "unconscious parts" are in place in the unconscious mind, a coalescing of meta-states that, when activated, produce the thoughts-feelings.

> **When a child focuses his attention on a single striking feature of an object or event, to the neglect of all other features, he is centering.**

Concentration: expanding awareness

In addition to *sufficient* cause, there is also a necessary cause that gives rise to limiting beliefs. The concept is one identified by Jean Piaget as *centration*. When a child focuses his attention on a single striking feature of an object or event he is centering. In doing this, children distort the contextual meaning surrounding the event because they lose sight of other perspectives. Piaget noted that younger children lack the ability to focus on more than one part of a situation at a time.

> **Children can focus on only one element at a time, to the exclusion of all other elements. Is this not the definition of a trance?**

Centration in action
A child watches her father become violent toward her mother. The child may see information just by focusing on the father's facial expressions of rage. Father's face, spewing out rage-filled words, may be the most outstanding part of the event, so the child centers on this. Before the age of eight the child cannot consider other elements. These unnoticed elements could include other people in

the room that can, and ultimately do, provide safety. These unnoticed features could also include the actual outcome of the mother's being safe in spite of the father's anger. But the child focuses exclusively on the father's face and rage expressed there.

The result of this limited focus is a SEE and a limiting belief. This limiting belief may be something like, "Conflict with others is dangerous, so never disagree." This limiting belief then acts as an unconscious part, directing future emotional states and behavioral choices. The unconscious part may take the form of always avoiding interpersonal conflict, since conflict seems dangerous. This child grows up to be one who overly cooperates and abandons her individual needs, highly conforming to others' requests.

Cognitive limitation is necessary in order to perceive an event as a SEE.

Cognitive limitation is necessary in order to perceive an event as a SEE. With expanded cognitive awareness the child could take into account the larger context, finding that the situation actually turned out safely, overriding the initial impression and trauma.

Drawing conclusions depends greatly on observation and comparison. The comparison process is what gives the observation its meaning. If a person takes a 100-item test in school and answers 95 items correctly, he gets an A. But the person taking the test might choose to focus on the five missed items. He could then feel bad because these five items stand out and differ from the other items. Emotions are negatively influenced when we focus on the discrepancy instead of the accomplishment. Noticing what's missing instead of what's achieved takes away from the opportunity to experience joy.

The test taker may find that answering 95 items correctly places him at the top of the class for that test. No-one else even got over 90 percent correct. Now how does he feel? Young children lack ability to widen their range of perceiving. This limitation also seems true for elderly people. Awareness of bigger and broader perspectives diminishes, as does awareness of details that makes the difference between situations.

Children seem to live their lives in a trance, pointing their trance at the most outstanding events.

Children under the age of eight apparently live as virtual learning machines. As we have seen, all learning takes place in a trance state. Children seem to live their lives in a trance state, pointing their trance at the most outstanding events. While this process greatly aids useful beneficial learning, it also works for the negative events and their detrimental, limiting effects on life. Given a natural trance state for the first seven years of life, childhood is a vulnerable and impressionable period.

The SEE is sufficient cause for generating a limiting belief. The necessary portion is the process of centering. Without the limited perceptual ability, any given event would likely not create a SEE. This explains how our most powerfully limiting beliefs usually originate in childhood. As they develop, children can "de-center". Thus the portion of the equation necessary for a SEE is absent, preventing most additional SEEs.

Without limited perceptual ability, any given event would not be likely to create a SEE. This explains how our most powerfully limiting beliefs usually originate in childhood.

Providing children with examples counter to their beliefs can diffuse or offset their misperception. Counterexamples work especially well with younger children, owing to their all-or-nothing thinking style. If enough counterexamples can be presented, or ones of sufficient strength, the balance of beliefs will shift. Also, we expand our cognitive abilities as we develop, so we can review our past and alter limiting beliefs created during childhood. We almost never generate a limiting belief in adulthood.

Adverse events in adulthood, without a negative precedent-setting event from childhood, are likely to be met with a resourceful response. This may explain why some adults handle a difficult situation easily while others crumble. Significant trauma in adulthood, such as natural disasters or significant loss, may provide unfortunate exceptions to this rule.

The precipitating event that leads a client to seek counseling in adulthood almost certainly has its roots in childhood. The current situation resembles the general dynamics of the childhood SEE. Centration brought to bear upon a SEE produces the limiting belief and unconscious self-limiting shift.

The function of all effective NLP techniques or any effective therapy is to bring about the opposite of the process that produces the supposed problem. If centering is the cause of the limitation, then its opposite will solve the issue. If "con" is the inverse of a process, then "con-centration" is the ability necessary to find relief. The purpose is to expand one's awareness. Expanded awareness permits the person to take additional information into account. Processing this new information, the client finds different points of view about the childhood SEE. New beliefs form. The end result removes the limiting belief, extracting the person from an unresourceful position. The client returns to awareness of choice and equilibrium.

Encouragement for this concentration ability comes through techniques of Timeline Therapy™, sleight of mouth, visual squash (Andreas and Andreas, 1989), meta-stating, or any awareness-expanding technique. By moving from small picture to big picture, the client includes more complete information. She can then get a better view. The NLP technique of visual squash, whether visual or linguistic in makeup, is a good example of producing a bigger and better point of view. Visual squash is like the geological process that produced the mountains of the world. Two apparently opposing points collide. The result is a higher plane and a new peak/peek, meta to the level of the problem. This new perspective results in new awareness about relationships between elements from past events. This eliminates old beliefs, forming new ones and altering responses.

Using traditional therapy, sufficient counter-examples can eventually combine, forming enough mass to outweigh the former belief. The end result is like weighing down one side of a belief seesaw with the counterexamples, elevating the lighter side (maladaptive state) to new heights (a meta-state). However, direct meta-stating, as described by Hall, is significantly faster than gradually accumulating enough counterexamples. Meta-stating will be covered in more detail in the last chapter. The gradual style predominates traditional therapy such as cognitive behavioral therapy (Burns, 1980).

Cognitive-behavioral therapy involves a two-dimensional approach. The first part involves exploring the client's beliefs. In particular, it involves exploring the specific structure of the beliefs
and the evidence supporting the irrational belief. The second part
of cognitive-behavioral therapy draws on the principles of behavioral therapy. Here, the therapist asks the client to go out into the
environment and behave in ways he usually does not. The client
spends several months accumulating sufficient counterexamples
to offset or disprove former faulty beliefs about self and life.

**Cognitive-behavioral therapy does not directly address
states of mind, but the ultimate purpose behind this
therapy is to help the client associate into states that
were previously off-limits.**

Cognitive-behavioral therapy does not directly address states of
mind, but the ultimate purpose is to help the client associate into
states that were previously off-limits. At a deeper level, the client
discovers that his desired state does not result in personal catas-
trophe, thus he becomes free to associate into the formerly
vacated state. The client stops living as if he were still in the midst
of childhood circumstances with the accompanying perceptual
limitations.

Evidence suggests that using meta-stating and NLP techniques
as condensed versions of the traditional cognitive-behavioral
therapeutic methods generates faster and equally (if not more)
effective results, by directly addressing the states from which a
person functions. Changing the state changes all the other factors
that affect mental wellbeing.

Piaget identified a total of seven cognitive factors that dominate
childhood thinking. We just discussed the concept of centration or
the process of centering, but there are six more influential
concepts that shape our thought processes in childhood. The
complete list of seven is below:

1. centering
2. egocentrism
3. inductive logic
4. irreversibility

5. transductive logic
6. thinking in absolutes
7. generalizing

Egocentrism

People never quite cease being egocentric. In Piaget's model, being egocentric means interpreting all events in terms of one's own subjective experience (Flavell, 1963). Young children generally lack the ability to step into points of view other than their own.

The egocentric child believes that everyone perceives the world in the way that she perceives the world. If her shoes are too tight, she believes everyone is wearing shoes that are too tight. When a young child goes to the shoe store for a new pair of shoes, she just assumes everybody needs a new pair of shoes. This process is like centering applied to self. The cognitive functioning level is innocent in and of itself.

Combining egocentrism with a SEE creates significant influence on belief systems that affect future decisions. The child personalizes the SEE and carries this belief wherever she goes, assuming others share the same belief. Young children believe the world exists only as they see it.

> **Egocentrism seems to combine an associated state with extreme generalizing. This process is like centering applied to self and then generalized to all people.**

Inductive logic

Along with egocentricity comes inductive logic. In early childhood, unable to perform deductive reasoning, children find what they believe is true for self and then generalize the belief to others. Fortunately, children develop the ability to dissociate by about thirty months of age. Dissociation, in this context, means the ability to step back from a situation and emotionally-mentally disconnect from it. They can dissociate an unpleasant act from its context. A child, having received a spanking from her mother, may soon go to a doll and repeat the punishment on the doll. Freud (1914) called this action *displacement*. The child is able to step outside of herself (dissociate) and apply her experience to another, be it to a doll.

The child dissociates, thus learns to disconnect from the first-hand experience. This principle of dissociating forms the foundation for play therapy with children. Whether the play therapy uses story-telling, sand-tray therapy, or another form of activity, it utilizes the principle of dissociating as its vehicle for healing. The child will not develop the ability for abstract thinking for about another eight or nine years. However, she can sufficiently disconnect from an event to make it second-hand.

Irreversibility

Irreversibility is also a trait of childhood thinking. Irreversibility means that a cognitive structure, once changed, cannot reverse itself. If perceptions were on a timeline, the child could not go back in time to reclaim a previous perspective, state, or belief. For those who are familiar with NLP, and in particular the fast phobia cure (Andreas and Andreas, 1989), a child is probably not able to perform the cognitive feat necessary for this technique. Generally, children under the age of six or seven cannot run their mental tape in reverse. Once a belief is formed, they can only move forward with that belief.

Irreversibility means a cognitive structure, once changed, cannot reverse itself.

The concept of irreversibility also plays a role in a person's ability to reach states of equilibrium. With the development of reversibility, the person can leapfrog over the limiting state and access a state of equilibrium, returning to a resource state that existed prior to a limiting state.

The natural dynamics of states works in favor of the person. For example, if you doubt something, then doubt your doubt, the two mirror images cancel each other. Equilibrium returns in the form of a state that may be called certainty or confidence. Doubting your doubt eliminates its influence. This process resembles the NLP "sleight-of-mouth" technique (Hall and Bodenhamer, 1997).

Essentially, negating a state involves bringing one limiting meta-state (a negative state) to bear upon itself.

Negating a state involves bringing one limiting meta-state (a negative state) to bear upon itself and can be accomplished with any limiting state. The equilibrium-restoring process follows the mathematical rule that a negative times a negative creates a positive. A positive (resourceful) state times a positive state leads to a stronger positive. For example, feeling totally calm about feeling totally calm only strengthens the positive state.

The process of inverting a state takes place when the client is asked to identify the state that is limiting and unwanted. The client is then asked to identify the opposite. This inquiry leads the client to the state that is the inverse. Inverting states can be accomplished with any negative state, paving the way back to balance.

When a young child operates from problem states that stem from a SEE, the state is subject to irreversibility. The child cannot recall the previous state. He then continues operating from this state or one even more extreme and further away from the midpoint. The compensating continues and contributes to maintaining the problem state and its accompanying response limitations. The child whose efforts at being assertive get squelched may react by becoming more passive.

Clients often cannot recall how they felt or thought prior to the state they use now in compensating for a SEE.

If a client does recall a state, the answer comes across as distant and almost like a guess. If the SEE took place in early childhood, a person cannot easily revert. Other cognitive skills are needed in order for the client to rise to higher meta-levels of mental functioning.

Once a child develops the ability to accomplish reversibility, he gains the permanent ability to return mentally to the starting state of any operation. Resourceful states that were abandoned in a self-protective act during a SEE can now be regained.

Children believe that events occurring closely together in time have a cause-effect relationship.

Transductive logic

Piaget found that children use a particular kind of faulty reasoning or logic during early childhood. He called this type of reasoning transductive logic. Children believe that events occurring closely together in time should be given a cause–effect relationship. This mental process exerts exceptional power and influence in shaping beliefs. Transductive logic makes for wild conclusions and bizarre cause–effect beliefs.

While all of us generalize, children lack necessary abilities for doing so effectively. Young children generalize in illogical ways. They rely on instinctive thoughts and appearances rather than judgment and reasoning. Seeing only a small portion of the whole picture, children quickly jump to conclusions. They reason from idea to idea or event to event without logically linking them.

Transductive logic in action
Transductive logic suggests that two events occurring closely together in time have a cause–effect relationship. Children may use transductive reasoning when explaining two time-separated SEEs. SEEs stand out from the norm and combine as a gestalt of events separate from the norm, a meta-stating process. The child weaves these SEEs into a single limiting belief and resulting state restriction. A child brings home bad grades from school and is harshly punished, creating a SEE. Then, a few hours later, his parents begin arguing with each other. One parent storms out of the house. Transductive logic links these two SEEs together in a cause–effect relationship. The child then forms strong but faulty beliefs, such as, "I made my parents get in a fight and now I made one of them leave. I am bad and I cause problems for people."

The young child cannot take into account the possibility that parents have issues of their own that drive these family conflicts. The child cannot consider other points of view. Using limited cognitive skills and faulty logic to find the common thread that runs through these conflicts, the child can draw only the conclusion that he caused these events, and he assumes the blame.

Owing to his egocentricity, the child cannot consider other points of view very well. He has only himself to find as a cause for explaining these events.

From this point on, the child may allow himself to associate only into those states that lead to perfectionism or highly responsible behavior. He may fear that anything less will result in a poor performance and cause conflict in relationships. It may seem from the outside that this child is a perfectionist in order to gain approval or prevent rejection. But he is actually rejecting states within himself that would allow him to be more at ease and relaxed. This perfectionist strategy is used to prevent conflict between others. The result is a highly productive child from a highly conflicted home.

Combining transductive reasoning with centration and egocentrism offers some insight into how children come to choose their personality.

Combining transductive reasoning with centration and egocentrism offers some insight into how children come to choose their personality. They focus on a single portion of an event, believe they caused it, apply this belief to self, and extrapolate this belief to others. Children cannot consider any explanation other than that they are directly the cause of events around them. This may explain why children avoid certain stimuli, because they believe it will lead them to associate into an emotionally distressing state. The result is that children choose states to associate into that they believe are safe and avoid ones associated with emotionally painful experiences.

Transductive logic and disequilibrium
A woman in her late twenties came in for counseling. She was a bright, college-educated woman. She was in a reportedly good

marriage and had a beautiful young child. Life was generally easy and there were no financial concerns. According to her, she had all the things in her life that she held as important but she felt quite unhappy. She was not just unhappy with her life but she was angry with herself for not feeling happy.

The client gradually unfolded a very strong and well-developed state of pessimism that she'd turned to as a coping mechanism in childhood. She revealed that her childhood was very tumultuous. Her father left when she was very young and her mother remarried, but that marriage failed also. Her mother was an alcoholic who eventually committed suicide when the client was only eleven years old. Adding more to the trauma, this eleven-year-old child found her mother right after the suicide. Now the only semblance of stability and constancy she had in her life was gone. Her grandparents took over the responsibility of raising her for the remainder of her childhood.

She felt that, every time things went well in her life and she felt happy, something bad would happen. Bad events followed the good events. She would then feel disappointed and sad. She decided to prevent these feelings of disappointment by adopting a constant state of pessimism. She reasoned that this way she could not feel sad. Her logic at the age of eleven was that her state of happiness causes these bad events to take place in her life. She had become phobic about associating into the state of being happy.

This client did not allow herself to experience happiness, no matter how well things went in her life. Her graduating college, her marriage, the birth of her daughter—all were met with the same state of fear-driven pessimism. She lived in a constant state of fear of what might happen rather than enjoying what was happening. This whole process was the result of childhood logic, concluding that optimism and happiness *cause* bad things to happen.

In therapy, she made great strides and eventually came to relish her good fortune. She made the changes through a variety of interventions that allowed her to override her early coping style and adopt a more effective one. One way to motivate change was to ask, "How does feeling bad keep you from feeling bad?" This addressed the very purpose of her coping mechanism and exposed its ineffectiveness.

After several therapy sessions she eventually reached a very welcome state she referred to as "happiness with a kick". This meant experiencing a little good spice added to the happiness, energizing it that much more. The relentless fear and searching for potential catastrophes were gone. She could and did enjoy what she actually had in her life at the moment. She reached a point of allowing herself to feel happy about feeling happy.

You can pay attention only to what you notice. And, so often, what you see in your mind is what you get as an outcome.

Pessimism increases the likelihood of the negative outcome. So often, what you see in your mind is what you get as an outcome. If things do go wrong after a promising start, a person relying on pessimism only deepens the pessimism. Things turned out badly because he didn't expect the worst hard enough! The only way this strategy can lead to relief is if things turn out poorly every time some goal is desired! The result is similar to a phobic reaction to the state of optimism.

States that are not resourceful must surely base themselves on fear.

Perhaps the emotions that make up optimism feel unsafe as well. If care and hope compose optimism, these two emotions would become taboo to the pessimist. Pessimists fear care and hope because they believe these two states caused bad outcomes in the past while they were associated into them. This same logic influences how a person feels about relationships. He may fear that he's going to get rejected and end up alone, so he never allows a relationship to evolve, thus ending up alone. Beliefs promote outcomes regardless of the belief.

States that are not resourceful must surely base themselves on fear. The child shifts away from a resource state after experiencing a SEE. This means that a person must experience a sense of safety in order to associate into a state. The idea resembles Maslow's basic needs of survival and safety applied to state choice. An absence of safety causes a shift to another state.

A child is usually willing to gain a feeling of safety in exchange for sacrificing desired outcomes. But this win/lose proposition (safety for limited success), with its safe but frustrating outcomes, eventually accumulates enough poor outcomes to turn into a safety threat itself. Depression also becomes a real possibility. The person choosing safety over successful outcomes looses some sense of fulfillment.

A person's cognitive level of development dictates his perceptions and beliefs.

A person's cognitive level of development dictates his perceptions and, thus, his beliefs. It also seems that primary states are more egocentric and narrower in awareness than meta-states. The primary states seem to originate during the time when a child is purely egocentric. These states are basic equipment. The multi-layered meta-states occur only after a child develops the ability to think about thoughts.

It seems that the ultimate meta-state of pure potentiality is the nonegocentric state. The ultimate meta-state has neither the cognitive limitations of a child nor the self-protective need adults satisfy from egocentricity.

Thinking in absolutes

Piaget (1965) found that young children think in absolutes. The child has no ability to compare items in terms of rank or relativity. Comparisons are made only in terms of absolute opposites. For every best, there exists a worst. No awareness of a hierarchy of values occurs to the child. Exceptions do not exist. If exceptions are noted, a new rule is created with the old forgotten. People or things are all good or all bad, slow or fast, best or worst. When personality-disordered adults think in these terms, it is known as affective splitting.

Generalizations

Young children generalize routinely as they have no cognitive option to take note of exceptions. They focus on similarities and find it difficult to do otherwise. Children lack the ability to hold two or more items in their mind at once and do a compare and contrast of the items. Children can think about one item or another, bound by thinking in absolutes, but not two or more at once until they reach about age seven. You may have experienced a child generalizing. When she first learns that a dog has four legs and a tail and the child then sees her first cow. She immediately points and yells out, "Dog". You then correct her by pointing out the differences between a dog and a cow. Also, notice that we adults generalize very well when we get in a highly emotional argument. Have you ever said or heard, "You never do anything around the house" or "You always get your way"?

Meta-programs

Meta-programs are information-sorting and information-filtering mechanisms. They operate meta to our senses and direct the focus of our attention. We sort and organize all stimuli we perceive through our senses. Our brain uses various methods for sorting. For example, when comparing stimuli we sort for their similarities or differences. We can tune into similarities between items or notice how they are different.

Hall and Bodenhamer identify at least 51 meta-programs within five broad categories in their book, *Figuring Out People* (1997). Categories of general meta-programs include eight processing styles such as sorting for similarities/differences. The authors identify seven feeling programs such as using an external or internal frame of reference in directing one's life (self-reliant/other-reliant). Additionally, they describe eight styles of choosing (e.g., preferring people, places, things, activity, information), eight types of responding (along the line of introvert/extrovert, for example) and eight ways of conceptualizing (such as whether we experience life primarily through our emotions, physical sensations, thoughts, or actions).

Meta-programs structure our perception of stimuli in our environment.

We sort information by matching select parts to a criterion. We ignore parts of any whole that do not match the criterion. For example, look around the room that you are in right now for twenty seconds and notice all the objects that are blue—any shade of blue, large or small, near or far—and then return to the text. Now recall how many red objects you saw. You probably remembered only a few, if any, red items.

Meta-programs sort through all of the stimuli in our environment with a particular purpose. While sorting for only blue objects, we exclude all items of any other color. With this criterion, only blue items compose our world, yet all other colors continue existing. Meta-programs shape the reality we experience and influence how we respond. While meta-programs limit awareness, all truths simultaneously exist. We just choose the ones we believe best serve our purpose.

**Meta-programs and the perception they encourage
play a role in solving personal problems, but they also
contribute to sustaining them.**

Problems result from two general mistakes. First, we believe our perceptions are completely true and, second, we forget other realities exist along with the one we perceive.

The original seven cognitive-perceptual styles identified by Piaget exert an especially strong influence on us. Piaget's meticulous mapping of these cognitive-perceptual principles and their dynamics assists us further to put together the puzzle of the human personality. These styles of thinking play a crucial role in the early shaping of personality. It may be safe to say that the basic meta-programs operating during the first seven years of life are the essential ingredients of most, if not all, problem states. In particular, I refer to inductive logic, centration, egocentrism, generalization, thinking in absolutes, irreversibility, and transductive logic.

When we associate into a primary state, unless the state is modified, the state functions at the affect of these early meta-programs. Primary states are those states of being that are about or in direct response to the environment. These states result from perceiving through our senses. Included in primary states are a host of emotions, any emotion that we can directly feel about an experience.

I suggest that when we associate into a primary state, unless the state is modified, the state functions at the affect of these early meta-programs.

For example, when associated into anger, the state carries with it impulsive urges that characterize early childhood development. Generalizing plays an important part of thinking that sustains the primary state of anger. When we are in a primary state of anger we do not say that person's behavior is stupid and they must be having a bad day. We say that the *person* is stupid.

We may also generalize in another, slightly different way. Thinking from the primary state of anger and its cognitive limitations, we may think that everyone treats us the way the offender did. Centration displays itself by anger that focuses so exclusively on the irritating event that we exclude contrary evidence.

Irreversibility makes it easy to continue dwelling on an event because we forget the state we were in prior to the adverse event. The fear that prompted the shift to anger remains. We lose awareness of the equilibrium state that existed prior to the upsetting event and find it difficult to focus on anything but the event.

Transductive reasoning also fuels the primary state of anger. We believe the other person's behavior happened because we were there when it happened. The event happened while we were there so it happened *because* we were there. Egocentricity is central to how transductive logic personalizes events. That driver changed lanes and cut us off in traffic. She did so only because we were there, not because she does this regularly anyway or because she was preoccupied on this particular day. We personalize her behavior and oddly assume her behavior was somehow triggered by our very presence, believing that the incident would not have happened if we were not there.

Thinking in absolutes allows us only to feel angry about her actions or feel the opposite of anger. This opposite state would be something like acceptance or approval, which is not likely to be the preferred choice in the heat of the cognitive limitation-induced "battle".

Thinking on the level of either/or, in even slightly threatening situations, very often leads to choosing anger as a response.

Egocentricity sustains the primary state of anger. This is accomplished by making the event a personal threat. Egocentricity leads the person to believe that everything happening is related to or about self.

Primary states may operate as a result of this cognitive set because primary states first come to be known to us during our earliest years. In fact, primary states exist as our only states for the first few years of life. The most we can do is dissociate and go to one level meta to the primary state. Therefore, the primary states come as standard equipment along with the cognitive styles identified by Piaget. These cognitive styles represent meta-programs or perceptual filters. Unless modified or amended, the primary states maintain their original limiting perspectives.

It seems that all limiting states, primary or meta, rely on the cognitive styles of childhood identified by Piaget. Limiting beliefs do more than just rely on these primitive cognitive tools. Limiting beliefs require this type of thinking to begin and remain in effect. Once these states are altered, the limitations lift.

All limiting states, primary or meta, rely on the cognitive styles of childhood as identified by Piaget.

Dissociating from anger immediately expands awareness, modifying the *state* of anger. In fact, our anger modifies into another state. A child can generally think in terms of either/or, so the choices are anger and its consequences or some state such as forgiveness.

Adults can explore the wide world of meta-states and choose the response state best suited for any given situation. This may include curiosity, acceptance, or generally being solution-oriented instead of self-protecting and retaliation-oriented. Primary states also modify when people associate into states such as patience, foresight, and flexibility. These three traits or states represent the three most immediate ways to modify a limiting state. Injecting these three states into a limiting state allows anger to give way to determination for a constructive solution or some other resourceful state such as curiosity or cooperation. A person can then shift to make his meta-state the state from which he responds.

The issue we face in life at any given time is not the problem. The problem is our perception and reaction to the issue. Our reaction is partly a function of our meta-programs. These programs determine the colors that tint our perception. When we operate from primary states, our perception is subject to the greatest limitations, thus limiting our resourcefulness. Primary states in their original form often leave people poorly equipped to manage life's issues. Meta-States[R] override these limitations, turning the tables and placing us in control of our perceptions and subsequent states. This change results in our perceptions stemming from our state. We can then choose how to look at something.

When we operate from primary states, our perception is subject to the greatest limitations, thus limiting our resourcefulness.

The most common exception to this limitation by primary states involves basic needs and survival mechanisms. Here, primary states may give us the necessary responses to ensure our survival, almost an instinctive self-preservation process. In this case primary states correspond to Maslow's (1962) first two levels of need in his hierarchy, survival and safety. But, when these two levels are the only two from which a person operates, she severely restricts her options.

A problem state limits resourceful responses. Each problem state, whether in childhood or adulthood, contains the cognitive styles identified by Piaget. These meta-programs cause limiting perceptions and result in limiting beliefs and unresourceful states. Problem states most often develop in childhood in response to a SEE. The developmental level and associated perceptual limitations stop evolving at the time of the SEE. A sort of defense mechanism determines that blocking further development better protects the self.

From the point of the SEE forward, the person moves on through time, operating from her arrested developmental level. She continues perceiving the original issue, and ones like it, as she did during childhood. However, this process of limited perception that gives rise to an unresourceful state, may also develop in adulthood under extreme adversity. Either point of origin carries with it some limiting perceptions.

A problem state could not exist without these limited perceptions. While meta-programs support and sustain any state, they limit progress in moving past problem states. Meta-programs, resulting from adversity or simply the unaltered perceptual style of childhood, provide the glue that holds a problem state in place. The perceptual set that is a meta-program serves to sustain a defensive state. This defensive state is designed to protect a supposedly endangered state.

Meta-programs, resulting from adversity or the unaltered perceptual style of childhood, provide the glue that holds a problem together.

A person adopts a state of aggression when interacting with others because he came to fear, from childhood experiences, that if he's assertive, people will overrule and dominate him. At the first hint that someone is trying to dominate him, he feels the need to shift immediately to the state of aggression so that he can take control of the interaction. He looks for, finds, and interprets cues in the environment to support his beliefs. Aggressive people also tend to utilize the state of paranoia to some degree as well.

After the encounter, utilizing aggression with another person, he walks away believing that, if he had not become aggressive, the other person would have controlled him. He finds this experience as just another example whereby his aggressiveness keeps him safe. Therefore, reactions to events actually function to sustain states. A self-sustaining loop develops involving states, meta-programs, beliefs, and behavior, sealing out any new information.

We usually find what we're looking for and react in such a way as to create the very outcome we expected. We twist the information we perceive (poor assimilating) into information that supports the state we occupy (poor accommodating). This perceptual twist happens because meta-programs necessarily paint perception in ways that support the status quo. Yes, it seems a conflict of interest. It reminds me of politicians: once they are in office, all their actions are designed to preserve their position.

We can react to events in the environment and allow our faulty perceptions to rule, or we can make a different choice. By choosing which meta-state we utilize, we can then choose the prophecy we want to fulfill.

Self-fulfilling prophecies happen regardless of what state we utilize.

The role of meta-programs in sustaining states is like an extreme version of Piaget's assimilating and accommodating concept. When we assimilate, we take in information and compare it to what we already know. However, meta-programs taint the information to support pre-existing beliefs. We did not accurately assess the situation. Better assimilating and accommodating would result in our adjusting to new information and updating beliefs. The result would be that one alters one's course to equilibrium.

The seven primary cognitive styles present in early childhood can lead to faulty conclusions about states. These conclusions dramatically affect the relationship we have with our states, marking some as off-limits and others as acceptable. This then leads to potential disequilibrium, and that makes for the inevitable struggle to regain equilibrium.

The childhood thought processes contribute to the construction of limiting beliefs and problem states. These problem states then play out in adulthood and sustain themselves by their own perceptual-cognitive set. Therapy can address any one of these cognitive deficits and begin to bring about positive change for the client. A summary of these cognitive deficits can be seen in Table 2.1.

The concepts used by Piaget equate to our window through which we view the world during our first few years. It seems all

Table 2.1: Cognitive styles identified by Piaget

Assimilation	Gathering ideas, information, perceptions, and experiences and then fitting them into existing maps of the world.
Accommodation	Modifying old information with new information to form new maps of the world, leading to new action.
Adaptation	Adjusting self to the environment as a result of assimilating and accommodating.
Centration	Focusing attention on a single aspect of an event or object to the exclusion of other important features.
Egocentrism	Interpreting all events in terms of one's own subjective experience, unaware that other points of view exist.
Inductive logic	Reasoning from a specific instance to make generalizations based on this single event.
Absolutes	Thinking in all-or-nothing terms such as good/bad and right/wrong with no gray area.
Generalization	Assuming events with any similarity to the original event are exactly like the original event.
Irreversibility	The inability to reverse thought processes, and their associated states, to the original form prior to an event.
Transductive reasoning	Reasoning that believes two events occurring closely together in time have a cause–effect relationship. Time is used as the logical link.

problem states, or states of personal distress, require these perceptual styles to create a "problem". These early tools shape our initial interpretations and beliefs about the world. Our response to the world is then based on these beliefs.

Chapter Three
Equilibrium Theory's Roots in the Major Schools of Psychology

In this chapter we will look at some of the major schools of psychology: psychoanalytic, cognitive, humanistic, and behavioral. Equilibrium theory draws upon all these schools. This leads to a unified theory that goes beyond the major theories. This section begins with the theories of Carl Jung.

The state-of-equilibrium theory parallels Carl Jung's (1953) work in several ways. Jung believed that the human personality contains the full spectrum of personality traits, not just the ones a person displays. Each person is seen as a whole personality. Jung goes on to say that, while we may hide certain personality traits from others or ourselves, we spend our lifetime striving to regain the original sense of wholeness as a person. This last idea plays a crucial role in the equilibrium theory. The drive to keep or regain and maintain states of equilibrium begins with Jung's concept of striving for personal wholeness.

The shadow states

One of the concepts in Jung's personality theory that relates to the equilibrium theory is Jung's concept of the "shadow". A person's "shadow" consists of the personality traits that a person feels are socially unacceptable. In Jung's theory, the shadow is the complementary version or the opposite personality trait to that which the person displays to society. For example, a person raised to be compliant and cooperative with others makes these traits his public image. At the same time he hides his individuality and assertiveness as his shadow.

Equilibrium theory suggests that in order to create a shadow we must first abandon the midrange of states and behaviors. By so doing, and going to one end of the continuum, we create an inverse set of states and behaviors as our only response options. The opposing ends of the continuum form the opposite to the middle. These opposite ends, then, are the states of disequilibrium, representing the only two response options available after we have abandoned the center.

When we believe that an equilibrium state is unavailable, the only acceptable alternative is either of its two extremes.

Now, faced with an either/or dichotomy (notice the thought-perception limitation that immediately happens after vacating equilibrium), the person must choose one of two less than effective response options. Let's use the example of a person who decides that utilizing the equilibrium state of assertiveness is unacceptable. This person must now utilize either passivity or aggression. Depending on circumstances, he may decide to utilize passivity. This choice sets up the aggressive state as his shadow.

After he has chosen either of the two extremes of a state, a line is drawn on the behavioral continuum: for example, a state existing on a continuum that ranges from passive through assertive to aggressive as being on a 1–9 scale. Passive ranges from 1 to 3, assertive from 4 to 6, and aggressive from 7 to 9. When passivity is chosen as the response option, the line is drawn at the point on the continuum between 3 and 4. This represents the limit of personally acceptable behavior, passive only. The range of 4 to 9 is now seen as the shadow-unacceptable behavior.

In his new concept of the continuum, any behavior even slightly beyond passivity equates to aggression. Even assertive behavior is now seen as aggressive. The person who chooses an extreme state, any extreme, then puts the remaining majority of the continuum in the category of dangerous and unacceptable. He sees the state continuum as all or nothing, one-third acceptable and two-thirds unacceptable. At the other end of the spectrum, a person may leave equilibrium and choose the state of aggressive at a level of 8. He then decides that the range from 7 to 1 is unacceptable. These states make up his shadow.

From this moment on, a fear of utilizing any response state other than passivity is created. Utilizing a state beyond passivity will lead to a re-experience of the original emotional trauma that made assertiveness taboo in the first place. Oddly, this passive person will behave aggressively before she will opt for assertiveness. Even when she wants to stand up for herself, she will resist behaving assertively. This resistance to assertive behavior will continue until such tension builds up that she leaps over the midrange of assertiveness.

While assertiveness is acknowledged, utilizing the state is seen as unacceptable. This perception leaves the other extreme state, aggression, as the only other possible response. She then utilizes this state. Strong feelings of guilt and shame often follow this uncontrolled outburst. These feelings sometimes lead to further narrowing the range of acceptable behavior. Only the extremes of states are utilized once equilibrium is vacated.

Jung stated that a person usually believes it dangerous to utilize a shadow state. People do their best to avoid utilizing their shadows. For example, the self-restraining person believes that, if he ceased his self-restraint, a total loss of self-control would happen. This dichotomy comes to his mind because he thinks the midrange of the state is not available.

Once a person develops a shadow state, the only alternative to self-restraint seems its opposite, a total loss of self-control. Not only does he restrain himself when it comes to self-expression but he also restrains himself on the continuum of self-expression.

They may even appear to be bipolar. They don't allow themselves to operate from states of moderation or equilibrium. Shadows are created when we decide a state of equilibrium is off-limits to us. But remaining within the midpoint allows a person to fluctuate within a safe and effective range of behavior.

When observing people who operate from states of disequilibrium, it appears as if they do nothing in moderation.

This is not to say that we only and always operate from the midrange of any state continuum. We sometimes choose to turn a state way up or way down. The difference is that this choice is temporary and purposeful and results in a natural return to center after a given situation passes. The result is a comfortable absence of a shadow and wholeness within as the person has full and free access to his entire self. As Jung (1953) stated, man needs to find a way to work with and accept his shadow in order to achieve optimum mental and physical health. Jung went on to state that, upon reaching wholeness, the personality is liberated, healed, and transformed, becoming an individual in the healthiest sense.

Cognitive theories and equilibrium

Some of the seven childhood thinking patterns identified by Piaget share billing as irrational thought patterns in cognitive psychology (Beck, 1976). Beck identified seven types of irrational thinking that are very similar to Piaget's categories of childhood cognitive-perceptual styles:

1. **Arbitrary inference:** Drawing conclusions without supporting or relevant evidence. This resembles Piaget's transductive logic.
2. **Selective abstraction:** Drawing conclusions based on an isolated detail of an event. This combines Piaget's centering with inductive logic.
3. **Overgeneralization:** The same concept and term that Piaget identified.
4. **Magnifying the negative, minimizing the positive:** Overemphasizing or underemphasizing one experience to support a negative self-image. This combines either/or thinking, centering, and inductive logic.
5. **Labeling:** Making identity statements based on a limited experience. It combines the processes of egocentricity and inductive logic.
6. **Personalizing:** Much like egocentricity, in that the person believes an event is some reflection on self regardless of the content of the event.
7. **All-or-nothing thinking:** Piaget referred to this as either/or and black/white thinking.

Centering revisited

Perhaps the most crucial element in this cognitive error collection is the concept of centering. This narrow focus is an essential foundation to irrational thought. The individual takes one piece of information out of context and draws conclusions from it. In a most general sense, personal distress comes from a narrow focus on the universe. It seems safe to say that the more distress we experience, the narrower our focus becomes. Conversely, the most general solution to personal distress comes from a widening of our focus. The bigger the picture, the less the distress. Eastern tradition would say that holding awareness of the entire universe all at once prevents personal distress. And yet this perspective is lined with cognitive concepts.

> **In a most general sense, personal distress comes from a narrow focus on the universe.**

Cognitive psychology believes these irrational thought styles lead to problems, but I believe they actually sustain the problem. Yes, an irrational thought-perception of an event gets the "problem" started. But the irrational thought-perception must continue for the problem to continue. The irony is that the irrational thinking that gave life to the problem sets up a defensive need that recruits and sustains irrational thinking. "Huh?" you say. Please read on and it will make more sense.

Each type of irrational thinking has a reason: first it serves as a defensive state used to shield from emotional pain, second, it helps avoid an "unsafe" state. But the shielding state is a personally-limiting state that endangers the person in a different way. The result is that, the more the irrational perception is used, the more it is needed to defend against the dangers perceived through irrational senses. Again, these thinking styles amount to misguided defense mechanisms: they create the problem and then lock out awareness of the resources needed to solve the problem.

> **The solution to irrational thinking is to inject broader awareness into the thought equation.**

The solution to irrational thinking is to inject broader awareness into the thought equation—or, in Piagetian terms, to *decenter*. Cognitive therapy (Beck, 1976) achieves decentering by altering perception. The therapist identifies a particular faulty perception, then identifies the supposed factual basis supporting the perception. The client and therapist then explore this supporting belief with the therapist providing alternative perceptions to help the client to adjust his perception. By altering perception we alter what information is observed and how it is sorted. This altered sorting process leads different meanings to become attached to the information. The new meanings will then lead to a different state of emotion and new responses.

Meta-stating

Cognitive therapy works to bring about change from the bottom up, changing the individual's perceptions of the environment in order to change states within that individual. While this technique often works very well, the therapeutic technique of meta-stating works from the top downward or from the inside outward. The state changes first, then alters everything in its wake, including perceptions, thoughts, emotions, and behavior. This order of change happens because Meta-States[R] modify all psychological levels below them. This ties into equilibrium theory in this way: once a person restores self to an equilibrium state, perception, beliefs, and behaviors naturally align, creating more resourceful lifestyles.

Cognitive-perceptual theories are by no means the only theories that address states. Many psychological theories address and incorporate the concept of states and our relationship with them.

Maslow's hierarchy and equilibrium

The need for safety seems to dictate which states a person will and won't utilize. A person abandons a state he believes to be dangerous and shifts to a state that feels safe. A person will return to a state of equilibrium only when he believes that state is again safe. This priority of safety as a criterion for state choice relates to the theory of Abraham Maslow (1962).

Maslow developed a hierarchy of human need and corresponding motivations (see Figure 3.1). The seven-level priority list ranges from basic physiological needs (food, water, etc.) through safety, love, esteem, cognitive, and aesthetic considerations and to the ultimate level, which Maslow called self-actualization. According to Maslow, we cannot pursue any need above the one not yet fulfilled. For example, offering new home furniture (aesthetic needs) will not matter to a person who has no food or shelter. First things first. A person will first seek ways to survive by meeting her physiological needs. A person will next ensure her own safety. She then moves up the ladder of needs one at a time if, and only if, she successfully meets the previous need.

In this case, safety relates to long-term survival and stability. If the food we get to satisfy our physiological needs is not safe for us to eat, we exchange it for food that we believe is safe. Meeting the safety criterion allows us to pursue needs that rank higher under ordinary circumstances. We cannot pursue or meet any other needs if the need for safety is not met. Safety acts as a sentinel for all other procedures. Applying this priority of safety to any and all states, we find that safety is the crucial criterion we must satisfy in order to utilize any given state. If we believe a given state becomes unsafe while utilizing it, we then disconnect from that state. We then choose the state that is most similar to the state previously occupied, as long as it is a safe state. Our goal is to remain as close to equilibrium as possible.

Applying Maslow's hierarchy to states theory a step further, we can see how the levels of needs in Maslow's theory relate to various levels of states within the individual. Primary states tend to concern themselves with basic needs of survival and safety. Meta-States[R] tend to concern themselves with higher-level needs such as belongingness or, ultimately, self-actualization at a meta-meta level.

Maslow's model may be a hierarchy of needs regarding how a person relates to states within herself.

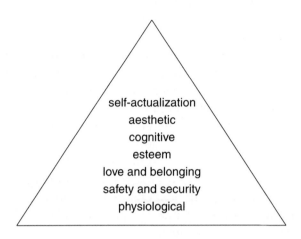

Figure 3.1: Maslow's hierarchy of needs

Maslow's hierarchy of needs may apply to more than the individual and her environment. It may also be a hierarchy of needs regarding how a person relates to states within herself. First she needs to make sure the states exist and tries out a variety of states just by experiencing a variety of life circumstances. Then she will need to make sure these states feel safe before continuing to utilize them.

Once determining a state or states to be safe, she will then move on to accepting these states and forming a more comfortable relationship within. She reclaims any formerly rejected states, and a deeper understanding of self happens as she gains full self-acceptance of the whole state constellation. All states or facets of self are seen as useful in some form or some context. The result is self-actualization, a true internal wholeness and harmony.

The equilibrium of Carl Rogers's self-psychology

Carl Rogers (1961) believed a person begins life with an intact and fully accessible whole self. Rejection or harsh criticism from significant others results in the child's hiding the part of self that he believed to be rejected or unacceptable.

Equilibrium theory follows this same logic but adds a cognitive-developmental-perceptual component in the child's decision-making process. Rogers said that the child then goes on living with a deficit inside himself, a disowned part of self. This resembles the equilibrium concept whereby certain personality traits or states are off-limits.

Therapy involved showing unconditional positive regard to the client, who gradually generalizes the newly received acceptance and regains wholeness.

For Rogers, therapy involved showing unconditional positive regard to the client. Receiving this positive regard helps the client form new concepts about self, finally accepting the formerly ostracized part of self. Rogers's therapeutic process starts from the environment, the therapist. The client gradually generalizes the newly received acceptance and regains wholeness. Until this therapeutic process of unifying the self happens, the life problems will continue existing because the client operates from states outside the equilibrium range.

Principles of behaviorism's within equilibrium theory

Lastly, equilibrium theory explains itself with some of the central principles of behaviorism. In behaviorism, the concepts of conditioning, second-order conditioning, positive reinforcement, and punishment combine partially to explain human behavior. Behaviorism states that a person will gravitate toward behaviors that bring positive reinforcement. A person will also theoretically avoid behaviors that bring punishment. In the process of his experiencing the rewards and punishments as behavioral consequences, certain stimuli become associated with the rewards and punishments. We then move toward the stimuli associated with reward or away from the stimuli associated with punishment.

Behaviorism in action–a personal story
As an example of these principles I'll tell you about my experience with two roommates during one of my years in college. I didn't know either of them before the school year began. They were assigned at random by the college. One of them became a very good friend and we were best men at each other's wedding. The other roommate was sloppy, self-centered, and spent most of his time bragging about his supposed accomplishment.

My friend and I were glad when our third roommate was out on a date or in class or otherwise out of sight. But when he was around us we found his presence a very negative force. In this case, the experience of being around him and being subjected to his bragging represents the concept of punishment. My roommate and I tried hard to avoid his presence.

Now we come to the principle of second-order conditioning. This principle states that a stimulus immediately preceding a negative or positive consequence comes to be associated with the positive or negative consequence. The second-order stimulus comes to hold an influence over behavior equal to that of the original stimulus.

Back to college now. This third roommate drank soft drinks at every turn. That may have been his most consistent trait. We knew when he was home because we could hear him in the kitchen filling a large glass with ice and then pouring a soft drink. This would happen just before he came out of the kitchen and into the living room to join us. The very sound of the ice cubes clinking together in his glass told us that he would be in the room with us in a matter of seconds. My friend and I came to dread the sound of ice cubes clinking in his glass. The clinking of ice cubes came to represent second-order conditioning since they were associated with his behaviors. The sound of the ice cubes took on the same negative power as his being in the room with us.

When a person experiences punishment or reward, the behavior is discouraged or encouraged, respectively.

These same principles of positive reinforcement, punishment, and conditioning play crucial roles in the equilibrium theory. But the factors are modified and under the influence of cognitive skills and developmental levels. In the theory of equilibrium, the state plays the role of conditioning. The conditioning involves the state the person utilized during the behavior.

He now believes the state is either good or bad and will either be drawn to or repelled by the state. This process happens if the person is still under the influence of limited cognitive skills and/or operating from the conformist level of development or below. He assumes cause and effect with the state causing the consequence. The power here is that the state is either punished, and thus avoided, or rewarded and thus attractive. But if the person is of advanced cognitive skills, no longer thinking from the Piagetian categories, then the state is not seen as causing the consequence. The developmental levels from conscientious and above also render the person and state immune to this cause–effect thinking.

Chapter Four
It Starts in the Beginning

The purpose of looking at developmental theories is to identify and understand the role of developmental stages in shaping our relationship with our states of mind.

At each stage of development we view the world and ourselves in unique ways. This perception influences our equilibrium.

Significant environmental events interact with our personal evolution to form beliefs about ourselves and our world, and from these beliefs we create maps of both the external world and our own world within. The timing of any significant event in our childhood greatly influences such beliefs. This influence happens because perception is strongly influenced by the individual's developmental stage. Table 4.1 and Table 4.2 provide an overview of Jane Loevinger's and Erik Erikson's developmental theories, outlining the characteristics of various stages. Each step must be completed before we progress to the next.

Within human developmental processes, a person moves along a continuum from total dependence upon caregivers to increasing degrees of self-sufficiency. Ideally, the caregivers provide us with food, shelter, clothing, and basic necessities. As development progresses, the child moves from physiological needs to increasingly external (less egocentric) and abstract needs.

As we evolve, we also shift from depending on others to meet our needs to developing strategies that enable us to satisfy our own needs.

Our physical strength, mobility, and intellectual and psychological evolution allow us to attempt to master higher-level needs. We proceed from symbiosis to individuality or separation as a unique entity. The location of perceived control gradually progresses from external to internal and self-directed. Others exert decreasing control over us as our self-generated momentum propels us toward self-actualizing (Maslow's ultimate state of development).

The developmental theories of Erik Erikson and Jane Loevinger

Tables 4.1 and 4.2 illustrate the theories of Jane Loevinger and Erik Erikson and show the characteristics of each stage. A corresponding list of dysfunctions that result from unresolved stage challenges is also listed.

Table 4.1: Erikson's model

Stage	Traits	Consequences
Trust versus mistrust	Infant learns to trust or mistrust caregivers, then generalizes	The necessary ability to form emotional bonds *or* severe restrictions
Autonomy versus shame/doubt	Development of self-directed behavior or severely stunted sense of self	Ability to access and utilize the self *or* likely personality disorder
Initiative versus guilt	Leans to balance own needs with those of others	A healthy assertiveness *or* co-dependency
Industry versus inferiority	Utilizes self-initiative or feels inferiority	Direct skills to achieve *or* stunts ability
Intimacy versus isolation	Develops intimate relations or is limited to connect	Maintains deep relationships *or* isolates self
Integrity versus despair	Life assessment	Content *or* bitter

Stages 1 and 2 of Loevinger's theory

The developmental theory by Jane Loevinger (1976) revolves around what she terms "ego development". That is the human

Table 4.2: Loevinger's model

Stage	Traits	Consequences
Symbiotic	Totally dependent on caregivers	Life or death
Impulsive	Acts on impulse, no foresight, others are source of consequences	Learn impulse control
Self-protective	Some impulse control, wrong is getting caught	Learn role of self or blame others
Conformist	Conforms to the masses, stereotypical thinking	Self or others as identity source
Conscientious	Internalizes rules and standards, empathetic	Self-directed behavior
Autonomous	Interdependence, multilevel awareness	Respectful of autonomy
Integrated	Integrated sense of identify	Cherishes individuality

ability to mediate between impulses and the demands made upon a person by the environment. The ego acts as a separating devise that allows complex thought to intervene between stimulation and response. Loevinger's theory considers the ego as the central element of the self, providing a frame of reference on the world. Loevinger believes that cognitive ability plays the deciding role in developing a person's ego or sense of self.

She refers to the first stage in human development as the *presocial stage*. Physical needs dominate this time period. The child knows no sense of self in the beginning of life. The inklings of a self begin toward the end of the first year of life. The self, in this case, exists only in relation to the mother or other caregivers. Since caregivers comprise nearly the sole source of reference, a child sees the world existing as either "self " or "not-self " (caregivers). Children live their impulses. They do not feel or experience hunger (separateness from impulses). Instead, they *are* their hunger.

The *symbiotic stage* follows the presocial stage in Loevinger's scheme. It consists of furthering the very gradual differentiation between self and others. Here, language plays a part in assisting the differentiating process. Children utilize their symbiosis to acquire some awareness of factors making up a "self" and "not-self". Language provides representative symbols for doing this.

The same process of using words to make meanings can be used differently to change a self-concept, freeing a person from self-imposed limitations.

Language and the meaning we attach to the words help to shape our self-concepts. Yet these words and their meaning are not carved in stone. These first two developmental periods in Loevinger's theory describe the child's development up to two years of age.

Erikson's stage theory

In Erik Erikson's theory of human development (1963), the person evolves or unfolds according to an innate plan with each stage building upon the previous one. Like Loevinger, Erikson also focuses on ego. He sees the ego as a selective, coherent part acting as a bridge between the person's inner life and his social roles. The emerging ego relies upon biological, social, and emotional as well as cognitive forces for its shape.

Trust versus mistrust

The first step in Erikson's human development scheme coincides with Loevinger's presocial period. Erikson refers to each stage as a challenge the child must master. He considers these states as crises. The first challenge in Erikson's theme relates to trust versus mistrust. This sense of trust develops at a fundamental level, depending on whether and how the helpless child's needs are met. Neglect or abuse by a caregiver will impair the child's ability to trust, jeopardizing the child's willingness to trust others.

Lack of self trust may damage a person's ability to develop and utilize self-reliance.

It seems this lack of trust in others extends inward toward the self as well. The adult, having experienced neglect or abuse in childhood, also seems unwilling to trust self. The state of trust actually becomes fearful to the person, resulting in a near phobia about trusting-both others and self. If self-trust is lacking then the person may lack sufficient ego to rely on for sorting information and decision-making.

A case study in trust
A woman who was nearly forty had a past of episodic neglect and abuse by others. Her abuse and resulting mistrust began early in life and worsened upon the death of her father. He was the only person she did trust. This loss seemed the ultimate removal of her source of trust. He died during her teen years. Her subsequent years included two divorces and a series of problematic relationships. Even her two grown children and her mother "took advantage" of her.

Dysfunction often results in making bipolar symptoms because the equilibrium state is believed to be dangerous, based on past traumatic experiences.

She gave of herself to others, yet did not trust others. She was a paradox of mistrust and gullibility. In her case, she could not occupy the midpoint on the trust continuum and, therefore, could not judge competently who and when to trust. Her internal map indicated that the midpoint on the trust continuum, the original state, was unsafe. She would alternate between extreme trust and total withdrawal from trust. Then she vowed never to trust again.

Her first challenge to recovery revolved around self-trust with the goal of eventually extending this trust, or good judgment, to others. Feeling trust neither for herself nor for others provided the point of therapeutic entry. She claimed she did not know how to trust. I verified this by stating she did not trust her ability to trust. With her agreeing to this, I then noted how she actually possesses a very deep and consistent ability for trust. Going meta (Hall, 1995, 2000), we found she implicitly trusted her ability to mistrust her trust every time.

The process of exploring the strategy she utilized in trusting her mistrust of trust eventually resulted in her reconnecting to a wonderful reassessment of her instinctive reactions. We found that her intuition was totally reliable at all times. In fact, the only times she erred was by not trusting her intuition.

This higher meta-program was gradually brought down to assist her in a more primary way in the here and now. The result was a joyous reunion for her, within her. She could now rely on her trust of herself in the here and now at the front end of an experience, rather than after the usual disappointment.

By contrast to the process that produces mistrust, caring for a child and nurturing affectionately leads the child to draw a different conclusion about the world. His maps of the external world and internal states differ from those of the mistrusting child. The child who is well taken care of draws different conclusions, or maps, about his first encounter with the outside world. He sees his world as one he can trust. Trusting as a state of being is then both safe and comfortable for the child. The result is trust of self and others in a reasonable way.

Let us look a bit more at the implication of early negative experiences on child development and the effect on the child's ability to trust others. It may be safe to say that relationships develop to whatever depth trust exists. If trust is broken in early childhood it may limit the depth of all future relationships.

People experiencing some significant forms of neglect or abuse during the first eighteen or so months of life are likely to display significant amounts of impulsiveness. At the same time they may exhibit strong desires to be taken care of by others and high degrees of dependence. This impulsiveness and dependence occur because the person has no place within himself or in others to utilize as a stable foundation of trust. He does not pause to look within for direction, nor can he trust others, yet he longs for others on whom to depend. An urgent search for trust follows in response to this dilemma.

Such people seem to be engaged in a search for, and yet feel repulsed by, trust in self and others. These people are frequently in and out of trouble with others and possibly the law. They may oscillate between helplessness and rage. At times their ability to form emotional bonds with others is impaired. In principle, the earlier the emotional injury, the more limiting are their relationships with others. The chosen compensation mechanism often leads to criminal behavior with thick personal defense systems, or the opposite: immense longing and vulnerability with virtually no defense. They either attack or become easy prey for attackers.

Loevinger stage two: self-protective

We move now to the second stage of human development. Loevinger (1976) refers to this stage as *self-protective*. The child evolves to further degrees of separation from her caretaker. We commonly call this phase the "terrible twos".

Additional development requires the child to become aware of boundaries: the self and the not-self. It paves the way for self-control and appropriate self-protection (boundaries) later in life. Awareness of self and willpower permits the child to protect herself from potential violators. Practicing saying no and general resistance to cooperation is essential for the future responsible use of those skills.

The child at this age shows anticipation of immediate, short-term rewards and punishment. Children begin developing a notion of blame but externalize it to other people or circumstances. They do not apply to self. Oddly, they may see themselves as causing others' behavior but not take responsibility for their own behavior. The self-protective child views right and wrong as a matter of whether or not others catch her. She believes she is wrong or bad only if caught, not as judged by some consistent external or internal standard.

The adult stuck at the self-protective level of development may live by the motto, "Do unto others before they do unto you."

Children operating at this level of development, or adults who never progress beyond this phase, likely display opportunistic styles of behavior. They may exhibit preoccupation with control and seek to take advantage of others. Some adults may live by the motto, "Do unto others before they do unto you." They tend to fear domination by others and thus can be prone to use pre-emptive strikes.

Erikson's second stage

Erikson refers to the second stage of development as a challenge of autonomy versus doubt and shame. At about the same time as Loevinger envisions, 18 to 36 months, the child increasingly expresses a sense of separateness. This plays out both verbally and physically. Yes, he says no. However, he also begins expressing curiosity about his environment as his mobility permits. The successful negotiation of this stage hinges on the parents' response to the child's ventures.

The successful negotiation of this stage, hinges on the parents' response to the child's ventures into an expanding environment.

The child naturally wants to explore the world and expand it. The parents can encourage and support this effort or discourage and disapprove. Erikson believes that praising the child's efforts and offering support provides a secure base from which to launch future explorations. When elasticity in the relationship with parents exists, the child is free to come and go regularly, within a reasonable range of space. In this scenario, the parents welcome the fact that the child is expanding and contracting her environment at will. They share in the child's enthusiasm and welcome departures from and arrivals back to them.

Parental resistance to or discouragement of exploration leads to a different scenario for the stage-two child. The result is some degree of fear, dependency, doubt, and shame. A quandary develops for the child. Either he follows his natural longings for expanding his world and risks parental rejection or gives in to the need for approval and acceptance. The influence of perceived parental or caregiver power becomes the determining factor. Children tend to believe that their continuing existence depends on their parents. The child tends to believe that, since parents brought him into this world, parents can also send him out—or so it seems to the child. As a result, the child may defer to parents' wishes. Certainly the child has no idea of the consequences that come from denying one's nature.

When a child experiences a significant negative encounter with a caregiver about the child's autonomy, the consequences can be quite serious. James Masterson (1976) theorizes that the syndrome known as "borderline personality" roots itself during the second phase of development. Stifling the child's drive for exploring apparently occurs during the process known as *reapproachment*. This dynamic, identified by Margaret Mahler (1968), takes place during the child's efforts to venture beyond the caregiver.

After physically venturing into new territory the child eventually returns to the parent, is *reapproaching* the parent. This serves, in part, to verify continuing parental existence and support, gaining approval for the most recent expedition and blessings for future expeditions.

According to Masterson, the child believes that he risks parental acceptance and, ultimately, existence, if he bucks parental authority.

The crucial factor in this process is the parents' response to the child's reapproachment. Ideally the child receives reassurance, acceptance, and support. This encourages further adventures. A child who meets with rejection, or negative emotions for his adventurous efforts, limits future attempts to expand his environment. According to Masterson (1976), the child believes he risks parental acceptance and, ultimately, existence, if he defies parental authority. This results in his sacrificing the development of self. A deep tug-of-war develops: honor one's nature and risk extinction or receive apparent approval for permanent self-restriction. The safe, yet restrictive, route results in extreme feelings of rage and depression within the individual. A sense of emptiness results from this self-abandonment. Any sense of self must then come vicariously. The result is neither acceptance nor a viable sense of self.

Loevinger's third stage

At the next level of development, Loevinger (1976) sees a transition point. If the growing child receives support and encouragement for further development, she moves from the self-protective level to a position negotiating entry into the *conformist* stage.

The child begins learning more socially acceptable behaviors in order to fit in with others later in the conformist stage. An emerging ability to delay gratification begins. However, the environment still contains the dominant power over the child. She takes what she needs from her environment by carefully selecting appropriate behaviors. As foresight develops, a corresponding increase in self-control occurs. The child develops the ability to string together successfully a series of behaviors designed to yield the outcome that she requires.

In contrast to the increasing internal strength, significant others successfully apply much external pressure, shaping behavior in accordance with socially appropriate behaviors. This process fits into Piaget's principles of assimilation and accommodation. These principles apply in different ways throughout life. The contents may differ but the dynamics remain the same. The child, at this level of development, assimilates the demands made by society to conform to social norms. He accommodates by adjusting his behavior to fit the demands, gaining approval from the group.

Swenson notes that a person experiencing emotional distress often responds by regressing to former levels of development.

However, if the child experiences significant negative emotional events during this period, the phase can last much longer. Swenson (1980) notes that a child or adult experiencing emotional distress often responds by regressing to former levels of functioning. She may also return to earlier ways of thinking, feeling, or behaving—such as lying or bedwetting—in response to stress.

When a therapist first meets a client, the client's functioning level is usually below his previous highest level. The client has not successfully negotiated the steps involved in achieving the next phase of development. Once he encounters adversity, he retreats to more familiar ways, attempting to introduce a sense of safety. The client's development is retarded until he perceives it safe to attempt the next developmental stage. Therapy can help the client to achieve this shift and find solutions to his problems.

Regressing is not necessarily all bad, if the time after regressin is used to develop a strategy to find solutions. This shifted focus takes the intervention itself to a level that is meta to the problem. Therapy focuses on whole solutions rather than the issues of the moment. Meta-stating (Hall, 1995, 2000), as a therapeutic intervention, leads a person to higher levels of cognition, emotion, and behavior.

These successively higher levels of functioning carry with them at least three particular qualities. Each results in greater degrees of foresight, patience (ability to delay gratification), and flexibility.

During the stage of development between self-protective and conformist, the child develops these three qualities. Development does not occur in an all-or-nothing fashion, so the child displays these traits inconsistently. As the child begins to discover the benefits of these three significant skills, the process of utilizing them results in larger and more important payoffs.

The development of foresight, patience, and flexibility allows the child to bypass impulsive behavior.

Instead, she can opt for what amounts to a meta-goal, superseding the immediate short-term goal. It seems safe to state that, when a child remains developmentally delayed, the type of behavior displayed, such as self-protectiveness or overconfor-mity, corresponds to an unresolved issue at this level of development.

For example, if an adult displays highly self-protective behavior then some emotional trauma took place during this stage of development. The adult then remains frozen at this developmental level until the emotional trauma is resolved. The same principle would then hold true for the adult who overconforms to societies' norms.

Erikson's third stage

We move back now to Erikson, and note that the period from the ages of four to six represents the next stage of development. He refers to this challenge as one between initiative and guilt, during which the child continues to be driven by curiosity. The range of the child's exploration broadens and begins to include people outside the immediate family. The support given by family greatly determines the extent of future explorations. Additionally, the child attempts to balance personal need with consideration of others. Social demands promote thoughtfulness of others.

In response to the child's dwelling on himself too much, the family may instill a sense of guilt in him for his "selfishness".

Assimilation and accommodation combine to develop a balance between self and others. If he converts the guilt into conscientiousness he may enhance his social skills. He can better take others into account in his decisions. But, if this guilt remains in its initial form of self-condemnation, he may limit the frequency and amount of future initiative, since he is so "bad".

The result of the initiative/guilt stage may play out in various ways. If he experiences overindulgence from the family and is granted total support for meeting his own needs, he may become self-absorbed and lack consideration for others. Sharing or generosity may not be one of his strong suits. He may achieve success in life but only at the expense of others.

On the other hand, he may feel guilty for even the slightest consideration of self if his parents discouraged him from pursuing his needs or encouraged him to feel guilty. This may play out in adulthood in the form of a person who self-sacrifices to his own detriment, stunting his own achievements, a co-dependent sort of person.

During this initiative/guilt phase of development, the child models adults as a way of learning more advanced behavioral styles.

Once again, parental response to this initiative significantly influences self-image and future endeavors. Ideally, they view exploring and learning as exciting and rewarding.

**When meeting with support and encouragement,
along with guidance toward improving performance,
four- to six-year-olds discover what they are
able to accomplish.**

Meeting with criticism and judgment from significant others almost certainly discourages confidence in future attempts. Half-hearted efforts follow and the self-image begins the downward spiral of a limiting self-fulfilling prophecy. It may lead children to worry or feel anxious about their abilities. They may hesitate in putting these abilities on display in front of others.

Beneath the surface of initiative versus guilt

We must look carefully at the motivation of the family in shaping the child when we examine this initiative-versus-guilt stage of development. Dynamically, the process seems similar to the previous Eriksonian stage: autonomy versus doubt and shame. However, the circle of influence has now broadened. The circumference involves people outside the parents such as siblings, extended family, and other significant relationships. The child ventures away from his parents further and for longer periods of time. Parents may assist the child in finding a socially appropriate balance between needs of self and others while the child expands the circumference of his environment. Parents and siblings may conspire to discourage the child from further environment expansion by guilting the child into submission. Rather than take initiative in the future, the child may defer to others on decision making.

In my work with as a counselor I have seen many clients who were the supposed "black sheep" of the family. A look beneath the surface of the family dynamics revealed an interesting family

69

code that bound the rest of the family together. This code said that all members must stunt their individual development, sacrificing individuality. Somehow the client did not fully comply and was given lessons by the rest of the family on how to feel guilty about his own natural development. It is not unusual for the client to be the highest-functioning member of his family of origin. The client was just wrestling with initiative versus guilt and didn't know it.

Co-dependency

Perhaps this is the point at which co-dependent behavior begins. If so, then the co-dependent adult likely perceives a dichotomy existing between behavior that she perceives as socially reasonable and that which shows no consideration of others. She may believe that, if she does not fully take others into account before her every move, then she is selfish and thoughtless. This thinking stunts proactive behavior. Not only is the point of view black and white, but the line of demarcation is so far to one side that the person severely constricts her behavioral options. She thinks something such as, "Anything less than totally taking others into account and obliging their wishes is selfish and inconsiderate." She uses all-or-nothing thinking as a tool for keeping herself constricted, lest she risk feeling guilty and possibly be rejected by significant others.

The co-dependent person equates acceptance from others with abandonment of self and her own needs. It seems that her all-consuming need is acceptance from others. This can only happen, in her logic, if she abandons herself and her own needs. Once again, we find an extreme behavior generating a shadow and the fear associated with the shadow. A shadow exists only when we depart the midpoint of a state. The extent of the shadow also exists relative to the *degree* of departure: the further the departure, the bigger and darker the shadow.

A shadow exists only when we depart from the midpoint of a state. The extent of the shadow also exists relative to the degree of departure.

The further the movement from the states of equilibrium, the more extreme becomes the behavior of the shadow and the more fear is associated with it. There is also discomfort with the compromises that would permit midrange or balanced behaviors. These compromises would involve those of thinking, feeling, and behaving. The person believes these are dangerous because this would place her in the state of equilibrium that originally proved so risky.

A lot of material has been covered in this chapter. So far we discussed the general idea of human development as a theory. We also looked into several specific developmental theories, their challenges and mental, emotional and behavioral consequences. In the next chapter we'll move to the other stages of development that span the rest of childhood and into adulthood.

Chapter Five
The Second Half of Development

In addition to an examination of Loevinger's theory at stage four, we will also look further in this chapter at Erikson's theories, and introduce some other developmental theorists and their concepts about human development.

Loevinger's theory, stage four

Loevinger (1976) calls the phase of development at the age of about nine or ten as the "conformist stage". Once again, the cornerstone emotion known as trust plays a crucial role in successfully negotiating this stage. The trust challenge in this case revolves around people outside the family. However, to reach the conclusion that others are trustworthy, children first have to determine whether their own family is trustworthy. Loevinger states that in healthy families children receive special status. This special status encourages children to decide that others can be trusted to treat them well. Parents doting on the child help to establish this generalization.

The conformist stage is characterized by black and white thinking about rules and the crucial decisions made during this stage. Loevinger believes that, during this age, the child can now consider thoughts about both his own welfare and the welfare of others. It is no longer an either or perspective. Complying with rules occupies this stage. Where the previous stage may have been typified by the sentiment, "How can I please myself?", this phase may have as its theme, "How can I please you?"

Acceptance into the peer group outside the family becomes of highest importance. Obeying group's and society's rules is done just because they are the rules. While the outward appearance of the conforming behavior seems to be self-sacrifice, it has its purpose. At the center of the purpose remains the need for approval from others. However, at this level of development both sides gain. Society gets an assistant and the assistant gets a society.

While conforming to prescribed "norms" may occur, individuality gets lost in the process. The child at this phase may blindly follow rules. Rigidity in thinking is probably present. One way of thinking about rigidity is that it is the process of looking only at behavior while excluding its intent. A child may reach this level of development and never progress beyond it, thus being a conformist throughout adulthood.

The rigidity of black and white thinking sees behavior as either conforming to the norms or not.

Many institutions in society function with a rigidity of thought. An example is the American public-school policy of permitting no drugs in the possession of students—zero tolerance. If the student is caught with any type of drugs she will be suspended. Conformist thinking and its accompanying rigidity call for no exceptions.

As a real-life example, a student brought her bronchial dilator inhaler to school with her. This inhaler is used to stop asthma attacks. The student with the inhaler loans it to another student who is in the midst of an asthma attack. The wheezing student had forgotten her inhaler that day. The loan of the inhaler to help with this serious situation breaks the no-drugs-at-school policy and the two students are suspended. If the behavior falls outside the prescribed rules, then the nonconformist receives the blanket consequences without looking into the details. Intention or purpose of the behavior is ignored.

While the conformist stage occupies a very important role in learning socially appropriate behavior, it can cause limitations if a person does not progress beyond it. Considering others in society is vital for society's healthy functioning and, indeed, for its survival. The person is dictated to by external standards.

Remaining at the conformist level breeds discrimination and clogs the creative channel.

In keeping with the creative process and conformity, I really like the definition of genius as the absence of fear. I heard this at the Tools of the Spirit workshop put on by Dilts and McDonald in 1995. No longer censuring ourselves with how others may react to our ideas, we become free to gain awareness of any and all possibilities. This position forces separation from concern over judgment or rejection by the masses. The guiding principle is that these ideas of genius promote the greater good of all.

Erikson's stage of industry versus inferiority

The next level of challenge, according to Erikson (1963), involves the child between ages six and eleven. The issue facing this child is whether to develop a sense of industry or a sense of inferiority. The arena for this scenario is school. Basing this stage on the skills and awareness from the previous stage (initiative versus guilt), the child attempts to display competence in new learning. As children learn how to harness their abilities, they channel them into classroom activities. They direct their curiosity and initiate their own activities. The children extend the first feelers designed for formal learning.

This process powerfully influences their self-concept. Mastering the previous stages in general, allows greater opportunities for future learning. Adversity at this stage may significantly impact beliefs about one's ability to learn. Peers begin to play a more important role for the child. Others are used as points of comparison. How does the child compare to the competence shown by others? Another ingredient in the process includes the standard set by the child for his or her performance. However, this standard originates with the parents and is made known to the child. Helping set the tone for constructive learning during this phase is the adage that there is no such thing as failure, only feedback.

> **At the upper levels of development, we use our highest purpose as a driving force, so that comparisons involve the individual and his movement toward his purpose.**

Each developmental stage replays later in life within different content. This stage of industry versus inferiority plays out each time we start a new task. Early on we test our beliefs in our ability to learn. We use our sense of industry to reach higher levels of accomplishment. We also tend to compare ourselves to others as we pursue our goals. Only at the highest levels of development do comparisons with others stop.

The roots of a workaholic?

It may be at this industry-versus-inferiority stage that the child first develops an affinity for or an aversion to the state we will call "satisfied" or "content". When effectively accomplishing a task, she may receive excessive criticism from a parent or significant other. The parent may point out only the part of the performance that came up short of perfection. Or the parent may silently withhold all judgment. This latter method often makes for an *obsessive-compulsive* person, driven to endless empty accomplishments. The child gets the impression that whatever she achieves it is never quite enough to get approval. As a result, she feels it is no longer safe to occupy the state known as "satisfied" or "content". Competence comes to equal failure. From that point she may increase or decrease her productivity.

> **The workaholic person may fear the state of "satisfied" or "content" as it stands for failure due to parental judgement.**

Therefore, the child believes she must achieve beyond a level of competence in order to avoid failure. The bar has been continually and excessively raised. Anything less than extreme productivity is nothing short of incompetence. And the moment extreme productivity is reached she must go beyond this or feel like a failure. Black and white thinking, as we can see, limits choice.

Little wonder the workaholic comes to dislike the person who finds ways to not work or drop out of society. This dropout person is his shadow. The dropout and the workaholic embody each other's worst fears, yet both are reacting to the very same internal conflict. They just choose the opposite way to respond to the problem. In general, the same root issue can have two opposite manifestations.

Interestingly, the same behavior can also have two opposite roots. Think about a person who is highly successful. This person may have two very different motivations at work: one may be to strive for success to avoid deeply rooted fears about competence—fearing failure, another may be to strive for success in order to utilize skills and find just how much can be achieved.

> **Interestingly, the same behavior can also have two opposite roots.**

How can you tell the difference between the two very different motives with similar outward manifestations? One difference shows in the reaction to success. The fear-based person finds no joy in success: "So what? You were *supposed* to succeed. Anything less is incompetent." The achievement-oriented person finds great joy in success. Another difference may come in the form of who benefits from the success. The fear-based person often designs her effort for self-gain. The achievement-oriented person more often designs her efforts for *all* to gain. Notice the two different developmental levels at work: the fearful one works from a self-protective level, the achievement one works from a conscientious level or higher.

To help us to understand better the way this single issue has two ways of manifesting, think about a person who used to work in a very productive way. She gradually drops out of society and is no longer a productive member. This dropping out may just result from a particular behavioral strategy. When a person who uses a style that tries to avoid mistakes makes a mistake, she maybe just attempts to do less the next time to avoid additional criticism. Is it possible that even those who are injured on the job and can't seem to recover sufficiently to work again are actually just displaying this strategy? I agree that some people do malinger, but this is a very small proportion of the population, less than 5 percent. The legitimately injured person may view her injury as just another mistake in a long line of failures. She may respond by narrowing her range of behavior to such an extent that it keeps her from working again.

Unresolved issues about competence within the parents may translate into high expectations of the child.

Surely the high or unrealistic standards "inherited" by the child must first come from the parents. What pressure must the child feel as she unwittingly assumes the duty of attempting to assist her parents with their unresolved issues? The child's effort at bailing out a parent's competence can easily lead to home and school behavioral problems. What degree of uncertainty would the self-doubting child experience when she finds herself in a situation that calls for increased self-reliance? She may seek solace or numbing from alcohol or drugs. How many "attention-deficit disorders" actually stem from and operate as learning anxiety or disapproval fear?

Scanning the horizon for possible dangers to self-worth may scatter attention, but attention is not at a deficit.

The child may feel like the young bird when it is time to leave the nest, believing his wings to be too short, too sparsely feathered, or riddled with holes. Should he just drop out or find a way to delay the believed inevitable fall? Delaying the inevitable fall (as he believes it) results in behaviors that prolong the worst possible outcomes—outcomes such as choosing substance abuse (and its consequences) or dropping out of school (and the consequences of undereducation). These sorts of choices prolong the very circumstances that the person fears: underachievement and believed incompetence.

The conscientious stage according to Loevinger

Loevinger (1976) sees the next developmental level is termed *conscientious* stage, and it can occur at any time after the person has reached the conformist level. The transition may take place during the teen years, later in life, or never at all. Some people remain at the conformist stage throughout their lives. Before a person can decide what is right for herself she must "try on" various values, beliefs, and concepts. As self-awareness increases, the individual recognizes the mismatches between prescribed norms and her own individuality. High school offers a fine example of when conformity yields to conscientiousness. A lot of experimenting goes on in an effort to find oneself.

> **For further development to occur, an internal gyroscope must emerge that allows individuality to take precedence over group acceptance.**

As the person moves toward the conscientious stage, she still must negotiate transition through the conformist stage with its need to belong. This need often leads students to join groups or cliques. The closer one is to the center of the group, the more intense is the pressure to conform and suppress one's sense of self. If a person has reasonably resolved the previous stages, he can do this. If not, he will feel compelled to continue seeking approval and acceptance through close group conformity. Paul Tillich (1952) wrote about the subject in his book, *The Courage to Be*. Tillich deals, in part, with the delicate balance between affiliation with others and respecting one's need for individuality.

Loevinger noted that during this conscientious period children gradually outgrow prescribed rules as they do an old pair of shoes that are too tight for growing feet. Priority shifts from emphasizing how others react to self, and moves toward increasingly altruistic goals. Decisions become guided by the ability to see beyond the moment and to predict how these decisions can benefit the greater good. People at this level of development see themselves as active choice makers in their own lives.

> **People at the conscientious level of development see themselves as active choice makers in their own lives.**

So-called advanced societies operate from this level. I believe a great need for safety may determine a decision to stay within a group persona. The individual may see much-needed approval available only within the group and not at advanced levels of development. As a result he freezes development at this level.

Other more unfortunate manifestations of operating from the conformist level, rather than the conscientious level, may include "hate crimes" and so-called "rebels". Hate crimes would be more accurately identified as fear crimes. People who invest in the "hate" group for life-giving approval and acceptance view individual differences as threatening and therefore bad. They project their fear onto people outside the group believed to represent the threatening differences. If "threatening" others can be stamped out, then perhaps the fear will disappear. This phenomenon plays out between individuals and groups as well as cultures and countries.

The "rebel" illustrates another unhealthy response to the conformity-versus-individuality challenge. This person is a conformist at heart who deeply fears rejection. Rebels enact the mirror image of the perceived norms, rarely initiating individual behavior. They first perceive the norm and then plot a course in juxtaposition to it. In their effort to achieve individuality, they actually leave themselves more trapped than the true conformist. If the conformist must achieve something, the rebel must achieve nothing. At least the conformist receives approval for her behaviors. The rebel must translate the disapproval into imaginary compliments for a performance poorly done or gain "approval" from other rebels.

If the conformist must achieve something, the rebel must achieve nothing.

The stage of moving from conformist to conscientious may be like the great divide. A person may decide to stay behind within the confines of conformity. But she may choose to brave the uncertainty and progress to the next level of development, becoming a free individual, leaving the limiting orbit of the group's prescribed norms.

Erikson's next stage: identity versus role confusion

The stage in Erikson's theory called identity versus role confusion corresponds to Loevinger's conformist stage. This is believed to take place between the ages of twelve and eighteen. During this time the child develops additional foresight. He begins to examine what he wants from life and how he may create this future. Exploring various ways to become his own person, he experiments with these during this developmental period. A sense of self is the ultimate outcome from this phase of development: who one is and who one is not. This notion of self and not-self is reminiscent of Loevinger's first stage of development, but the content is broader and more advanced now. The not-self is made up of parents but also extended family, authority figures, and peers—the larger society.

If a child grows up feeling acceptance from caregivers, he has a foundation of trust, autonomy, and initiative and a sense of industry.

The image of his place in the world begins to emerge. Erikson sees this as the most pivotal period to negotiate in order for the remainder of adulthood to be satisfying. It is, in effect, the young person's launching pad into adulthood. A sense of prior resolution propels the young person to greater heights.

However, with previously unresolved issues weighing heavily, one's rise to adulthood may be stunted. This may result in a feeling of being adrift as an adult and "playing" a role rather than simply being one's true self. Vocational confusion may also occur when children do not successfully tap their deepest awareness of who they really are and how they want to display this personally and vocationally.

For Erikson, each stage of development represents an ever-widening circle, or sphere of influence and interaction, within the environment. It progresses from self to parents to family as a whole, then to peers and now to the world at large. Each widening of the circle seems representative of the initial process of extending beyond what is known to gradually mastering the unknown. This ever-expanding environment is similar to the individuation process described by Masterson (1976) in principle, but applied to ever-enlarging arenas. Any stage where discomfort lingers has lasting effect on further successful development. You're ten miles from home and the wondering distracts you from focusing all your energies on the task at hand.

Unresolved developmental-stage issues result in a feeling such as the one you may get after you leave your house and don't remember whether you locked the front door.

Each stage plays a crucial role. Rarely does a person operate completely and only at one developmental level, because we are usually a blend of levels. We tend to develop in the way an ameba moves forward—in a piecemeal fashion using pseudopodia. But it is safe to say that wherever there is a developmental lag there resides an unresolved emotional issue.

You can think of development as similar to building a house. The first step is getting the raw materials, such as the concrete for the foundation (trust). This serves as the support for all future building. Next, you might collect the wood you will need for the general structure and its eventual details. You then get tools, such as various types of saws that allow shaping the raw materials into suitable sizes and shapes for specific structural parts (autonomy). Additional materials, such as nails and hammers, come next, allowing the structure to become more complex (initiative).

Once framing occurs, the plans call for aspects such as outer walls and inner walls (industry). Eventually, the structure takes shape and has an identifiable appearance with both external and internal identity. The added details make for a now livable structure. Life accomplishments then happen from this place. If, at any one point, either materials or tools are absent or deficient, the project is stalled or compromised from the original project. This is the case with human development, as Erikson sees it.

The autonomous stage

According to Loevinger's (1976) scheme, if development continues to the fifth stage, one reaches the autonomous level. Here, human diversity is not just tolerated but celebrated and held as precious. People are recognized as being different and this difference itself is very much embraced for how it contributes to enriching life. In earlier levels of development, differences are seen as bad or threatening to self. The autonomous person begins embodying greater objectivity along with the ability to recognize complexities and paradoxes in life. Also developing is a tolerance for, rather than a fear of, ambiguities. Awareness and appreciation of human interdependence manifests during this phase. Independence and cooperation now coexist comfortably, creating equilibrium.

At this level, the person no longer feels a need to prove competence. Competing with others is seen as detracting from further self-evolution. Mastery of self rather than mastery of others becomes the goal. The shame that often permeates the conformist level and the guilt coinciding with the conscientious level have vanished. The person in the autonomous stage may become aware of rather acute inner turmoil as focus now fully shifts from external solutions for internal issues.

With external influence now absent, the person neither feels obligated to resolve inner conflicts according to others' expectations nor attempts closure by projecting inner conflicts out onto other people. Such people know the issue is their own and they take responsibility for it. Additionally, they also know they possess the internal resources needed for solutions. The result is a greater feeling of control, more than any external playing out of conflicts could ever yield. The battlefields have always been within. Until one acknowledges where these conflicts exist, no resolution can occur. The road to true interpersonal and intrapersonal peace has now been identified. This road exists on the map of the internal territory, the relationship with one's states, rather than the map of the external environment.

Until one acknowledges that the emotional battlefields exist within, no resolution of the conflicts can occur.

The person at the autonomous stage develops a sense of identity. Those not doing so feel isolated. They may feel they have no one in this world but themselves. This feeling promotes a self-protective mechanism. Having yet to know who we are, how can we risk endangering the frail seedlings of hoped-for identity? I suggest the root issues resulting in isolating oneself reside in the more distant past rather than just the previous stage. Perhaps the person progresses, but likely by limping along. An earlier wound still needs healing.

Resolving conflicts from previous stages

As with most unresolved conflicts, two types of unsuccessful response usually occur in an attempt to resolve them. These ineffective attempts come from the by-product of conflicts from the past and often manifest in opposite forms in the present. The two usual responses are that people seem either to turn up or turn down the volume on certain behaviors in response to conflict. This "conflict" results when a person perceives the midrange of behaviors on a continuum as unavailable or to be avoided. One version can result when a child has been discouraged from *taking* initiative during the stage of *developing* initiative. One person may respond by retreating and not utilizing skills such as assertiveness and proactivity. The result is a passive person who defers to others in decision-making.

The opposite response may come from another person who experiences the same issue but in a different family. Instead of responding in a passive manner, as in the example above, this person responds in an aggressive style. Each of the two people views the state of equilibrium, assertive, as unacceptable. One responds with passivity and the other with aggression, but the original issue is identical for each. To resolve the "problem", one needs to turn up the proactive behavior and the other needs to turn it down. They will then converge at the state of assertive.

This response pattern, of turning ongoing behavior up or down, is similar to what's known as first-order change (Watzlawick, 1974). Here the person responds to challenges by just doing more of what she was already doing, even though the current response strategy is not working.

These seemingly opposite people, the passive and aggressive, often end up together in a relationship. They share a common unsettled issue from the past and attempt opposite means of resolving their conflicts. It is as though each had a different leg ailing, thus limping on opposite sides. By pooling their "good legs" they believe they will feel complete again.

Instead of leading to wholeness or freedom, the coping method actually prevents it. Neither party can now change lest they unbalance the fragile relationship upon which they believe rests their wholeness. Additionally, they now resist tending their own wound, thus avoiding a solution.

While each person is motivated to feel whole, the actual result of this effort is more like a three-legged race at the family picnic, awkward, limiting, and bound for a fall.

People seeking protection of their fragile emerging identity by using a passive strategy may also resort to remaining isolated. The purpose is to encourage further development, or at least preserve what is present. However, the original conflict around which the disequilibrium revolves must reach resolution, or else the person risks stagnation at that isolated position.

Regardless of how much identity exists, if the person does not feel a sense of resolution about her identity, she will continue to seek external solutions and will thus feel vulnerable. The vulnerability happens because she relies on others for her identity. This makes her identity a temporary and tenuous arrangement. The result is a perpetual loop of supposed development, reapproaching others, perceiving rejection, or loss of identity, and withdrawing.

Anything other than an internal healing of the conflict amounts to the same process of being insufficiently equipped to find and maintain satisfying relationships. The person then perceives rejection or inadequacy when the attempt to establish satisfying relationships does not succeed. It is as though this person believed that a certain developmental leash exists during a point in her development. This leash limit can be felt at any stage of development.

Variations in the reapproachment theme occur in increasingly larger venues as she moves from self to parents to family, peers, intimate relationships, career, and possibly society at large. This limiting leash prevents access to solutions residing in further development. In general, she believes she cannot further develop until she solves some "problem", yet actually she cannot solve the "problem" until she further develops.

This notion of not being able to develop unless you proceed to the next level seems, on the surface, to contradict what I've already said. I said that a person can't proceed to the next stage of development unless she resolves current issues. True enough in one sense.

Often people try to resolve the current issue with first-order change, more of the same, so an escalating behavior-consequence loop develops.

Higher-level thought: the conflict solution

The lasting resolution and development comes from elevated thinking applied to an old issue. This leads to a new perspective and further development, a letting go of the old issue. Searching for and finding new internal resources leads to change—the difference is the difference. To this point one has been searching for and not finding external resources.

Sometimes a person trying to gain a sense of identity through external means uses first-order change to gain this sense of identity. Remember, first-order change just means the behavior used is more of the same. If a person longs for a sense of identity it may be possible to have some identity by living vicariously. In essence, he borrows, or absorbs by osmosis, the identity of those around him. As a result he believes he must be around others as much as possible. Such a person may select one particular identity in line with his desire. He may also simply settle for the identity of whoever is around him.

In the absence of others, a feeling of being lost and some fear about this lost feeling then sets in. Sometimes the person using this style to an extreme is known as a *borderline personality*. Most often these people are attracted to others with an overpowering or forceful identity. This forceful one requires others to conform to her identity. Sometimes these overpowering types are known as *narcissistic* personalities.

Risks abound with the strategy of borrowing an identity from another person. Often, an individual with an especially amplified or flaunting self only wants to verify his own worth. The overt, forceful person may measure self-worth by how many and how much others follow in his footsteps. The identity-less person can tag along but cannot expect any accolades or a share of the spot-light. In extreme examples, we find cults, one "strong" leader with a following of others who hunger for a sense of self and belonging. The leader will give them this sense of belonging in return for obedience and loss of self. What seemed promising in the beginning becomes a dead end.

William Perry: development during college years

Before we go any further with the discussion of lifetime human development, let's look at the lifework work of the counselor, researcher, and theorist, William Perry. I find his decades-long work, which addresses human development during the college years, insightful, thorough, and personally inspiring. Having read several of his works during a particularly pivotal time in my own development, I find they hold special significance to me. Through his insight and foresight I became aware of existing at only a point on a continuum at any time in my life. I came to real-ize that there is always more and that I am always more than where I am.

While Perry's (1970) counseling and theory focus on college-age students, the relevance here is the common thread running through all developmental theories. Evidence continues mounting to suggest development moves from a constricted awareness to a more encompassing awareness. There is a letting go of the old in order to have more. While some sense of grief accompanies this letting go, so much more awareness and ability becomes available to take its place at higher levels of development.

Meaning makes the difference

In Perry's scheme, and all developmental theories, the meaning an individual attaches to any event generates all the power. Once again the only thing that happens to us is our thoughts. The overriding challenge during development relates to whether, and how much, a person accepts the responsibility for directing his life. To what degree does one acknowledge and deal with the unknowns of life? The individual moves away from humans as the source of answers and toward exploring uncharted waters. Fear plays a mediating role. The result is vast increases in useful information. However, the person must leave behind fear in order to commit to this process.

> **Rather than live in the past, the person moves, through continuing development, toward tolerating ambiguity and diversity.**

Development as external focus

Another measure of development is the degree to which a person is able to focus outside of himself. The further developed the person, the more he can reach outside of self and assist others or promote development in others. Focusing on others is not done in the style of the co-dependent person who self-sacrifices in the process. This healthy focus on others is all-inclusive and more of a sharing than a sacrifice.

We begin seeing how development unfolds as a natural path for people to follow. It is as if a magnet were drawing us to higher levels of evolution. Have you ever noticed how the view changes when seen from a higher perch? With each new phase of development, perception becomes clearer. The only block to further progress arises from perceiving unfinished business in the past. Developmental theorists believe that resisting growth causes more distress than going forward with the natural flow.

Ways of stalling growth

Perry (1970) notes three particular strategies for stalling growth. The first method is known as *temporizing*. This amounts to collecting more steam for forging ahead up the hill in the future. The collecting and contemplating may last a year or more. This temporizing is a pause in development with the purpose of gaining the necessary resources to forge ahead.

The second and more limiting style of stalling growth is called *retreat*. In this method people permanently entrench themselves in a black and white perspective about life. The fear of uncertainty becomes so overwhelming they revert to simpler forms of sorting. This is forced fit. This mentality is similar to Loevinger's (1976) conformist stage.

The final method for staving off further development is known as *escape*. The fear-based emotion of anger permeates this strategy. This is a permanent method for exploiting development. Rather than pass through a particular stage, the person allows earlier established opinions and initial separation from others to become obstacles to growth. The person clings to these supposed identity-giving thoughts as excuses for progressing no further. Her limited individuation becomes her tightly defended island. The person using the escape strategy views any new concepts as threats to her own security. Cynicism and paranoia characterize this position. A saying commonly used by this person is, "Opinions are like assholes: everybody's got one."

The person using the escape strategy views any new concepts as threats to her own security.

Beyond the measurable milestones of development resides an abstract element within Perry's theory. He believes that, with further development, we reach a point where we give up what we "know," realizing instead that we really "know" very little with any certainty. This nicely illustrates the process we all go through in moving out of the darkness into the infinite light. If we fear losing this or feel it absent, we will seek it. The solution or problem comes from where we seek it, within or without.

The fuel for moving forward consists of security and safety accrued and internalized from previous stages.

Very often we believe the solution to our past conflicts *resides* in our past. As a result, we attempt to replay scenarios with certain significant people in our life, or reasonable facsimiles, with whom the conflict originated. The past seems to be where we started utilizing the state or states we do not like. It is also where we remember last having utilized the states we felt good about.

In some way we then try to interact with the person in question in the same old style and yet end up with a new outcome. We may even behave differently in the fervent hope this person will in turn also behave differently. But this logic is based on two faulty original assumptions: one is to believe that the other person caused our uncomfortable state and so can alter it, the second is the belief that we can cause or alter the other person's chosen state or style of behavior.

Blindly re-enacting the past to create a new outcome will not bring the outcome we seek. The spilt milk over which we cry has long since evaporated. The solution to our past always resides in our present and in knowing that the future holds a new present awaiting us. Oddly, we fear letting go of our distress, since it has become equated with some sort of protection device.

In the process of personal growth, we actually reach a place of being afraid *not* to be afraid. This is a very powerful dynamic. What was once a protective blanket of fear has become smothering. But we seem to believe that letting go of the fear will fling us from a safe, albeit limiting, orbit, into the infinite unknown. We then hold onto states of fear or distress that seal us in the past while the solution awaits us in the present and future.

It seems to be the last and most challenging step of therapy,
releasing the fear of releasing the fear.

Perry goes on to illuminate poignantly the feeling of loss accompanying growth. He refers to "taking a step into aloneness". We do this in the process of leaving behind our concepts or beliefs and possibly some relationships. However, what new ones will we find? Accomplishing this progress requires an awareness that one can internally direct one's own states. Some fairly well-developed sense and operation of self must exist if one is to master this step. Self is defined as one's deepest, most individual resources. Accessing and utilizing this self must occur in order for us to step into the great unknown.

Connecting to separate to connect

This process of connecting only to separate and connect again, but in a different way, often plays out within groups of people. At a subconscious level, group resistance toward members attempting progress is common. Group dynamics adhere to certain principles. Unfortunately, these sometimes include discouragement of growth, which may be through the exposure of others' feelings about their own personal evolution. In some way, the remaining members may feel rejected by the dissident and, in turn, attempt to discourage her from leaving them behind.

Another dynamic may also happen to lead a group to discourage an individual's growth. As one individual grows personally, it heightens the others' awareness of issues they had been trying to keep from their awareness. The dynamic may result in some kind of mutual sensing of simultaneous abandonment. The individual senses his growing aloneness and the group senses that it is being left behind. This may separate the growing member from the group if the group lacks enough flexibility and tolerance of individual differences. All-or-nothing thinking may rule and result in a rejection of the unique member.

In contrast to this, positive group loops do occur. These groups value personal growth and promote it. The result is that members are inspired to progress as individuals, which promotes the other members' growth. Personal growth and group development take priority over conformity, in the knowledge that all members stand to gain.

Human development occurs throughout our lifetime unless we put up barricades.

The integrated stage of development

Development does not occur only to people under the age of 22. It occurs throughout our lifetime unless we put up barricades. Loevinger (1976) refers to the autonomous stage as progressing to the sixth stage of development, the integrated position. At this level, people have resolved many of the various demands of life. They cherish and appreciate the individual differences in people. They are nearly, if not quite, whole. The former unconscious parts that splintered off earlier have now blended into a larger whole.

As a result of the internal merger, perception of reality is clear and the person's response repertoire is larger. Along with a clear sense of self, an ability to give to an idea outside of oneself is present. This occurs as a by-product of a health identity. We can then go on the offensive. The offensive in this case means contributing to the greater good, the whole of which we are part.

Knowing who we are permits us to drop our defense mechanisms because we know our self is intact and safe no matter where we go or what we do.

Generativity versus self-absorption

Erikson (1963) also sees human development as continuing across the lifespan. Generativity versus self-absorption is the next stage in his theory. Once identity, family and career establish themselves, the person faces the challenge of an internal versus external focus of energy. Like Loevinger, Erikson describes the developing capacity of looking outside oneself as the ability to empathize with others. This willingness springs from successful resolution of previous crises. Settling internal conflicts frees the person to aim efforts aimed toward the greater good. The person effectively resolving the generativity crisis makes a decision to give back to the community or society at large. This person makes contributions for the next generation of people who will occupy her role. She attempts to make the world a better place than it was when she got there.

Passing the water pitcher to the next person is difficult when we have yet to quench our own thirst.

Unresolved internal conflicts at this stage make for a self-absorbed style, limiting ability and willingness to extend outside of self. Focusing on unfulfilled needs makes for a self-absorbed person. What we don't consider is just how many of our own needs we can satisfy by fulfilling the needs of others. Otherwise, desperation may set in and result in rather extreme measures to fulfill the longings, as time to succeed seems to be running out. The person in the unresolved position experiences a widening gap between what he wishes to happen and what seems to be actually happening.

Midlife crisis

This is the stuff of which midlife crises are made. Typically, if the scene doesn't involve a middle-aged man, a sports car, a younger woman, and a lawyer, it's not a midlife crisis. This sort of midlife crisis does not fit into Erikson's theory. For Erikson, a midlife crisis is one of accurately realigning with one's core values. Essentially, the person's outdated and dysfunctional beliefs have run their course. It now becomes time to release them and access the freedom that the "true" self brings. The weary defense army, swords dull and guns out of bullets, becomes too tired to fight. Now that the war is over, they need retraining.

Integrity versus despair

The final stage of development, according to Erikson, involves integrity versus despair. This phase involves comparing actual life accomplishments with longstanding values. You might think of it as being like an ecology check run on your past. It is similar to Carl Rogers's (1961) concept of "ideal self". The amount of discrepancy we find determines the amount of distress we feel. If we spent our lives pursuing what we held as important, then a feeling of satisfaction occurs. We are living a life of integrity. "Fighting the good fight " is more important than the specific results of the fight.

How closely have we lived up to the ideals we hold for ourselves, and how much like our ideal self did we become?

If we look back and find we lived a life that was untrue to our values, it may leave us feeling despair. Finding we were too rigid in living our values may also leave us with a sense of despair or lost opportunities and grief. Rigidity, rather than purpose, may dominate. The specific may dominate the general, rather than the inverse. Rigidity looks at the specific elements rather than their purpose. The sooner we recognize the core issues and their solution, the sooner we can replace despair with integrity. Rigidity prevents opportunities for fulfilling experiences.

With human-development theories now explored, we can identify three crucial factors influencing the evolution of our thoughts, emotions, and behaviors: cognition, social interaction, and "sense of self". Providing the platform for all development is our cognitive capacity. This collection of age-related perceptual filters determines our maps of the external and internal world. We know that these maps then influence our beliefs and behavioral decisions. Through Erikson's (1963) social-interaction stages of development, we attempt to develop trust, autonomy, initiative, identity, and eventual integrity.

Mastering the developmental steps becomes very difficult if emotionally traumatic events happen during them. However, these events are subject to interpretation as a function of the child's limited perceptual skills. The interpretation may have a more pro-found effect on future functioning than the event itself. Because it provides the basis for beliefs about self and world, the interpreta-tion, not the event, makes the difference. It is not what happens to us that matters: it is the meaning we attach to it and the response we make.

This interpretation of what happens allows a therapeutic opening for positive change because the interpretation itself is up for inter-pretation. The event is just a sequence of behaviors or actions, but the interpretation of the facts is itself anything but a fact. This is where choice comes into play. Limiting beliefs that develop in childhood result from limited perceptual abilities.

**The real problem resides with perception and
not the individual's beliefs about self.**

The gradually emerging sense of self may only partly result from the cognitive processing of social interactions. We need the skills of and states of trust through identity in order to develop a stronger, more defined sense of self (ego, in Loevinger's theory). We may rank the influence, from most to least, of these three shap-ing factors as cognition, social interaction, and sense of self. Cognitive processes either limit or clear the way for further self-development, everything else follows after.

Social interaction and its contents provide the fodder for personal development. Sense of self moderates what the person chooses in life but sense of self is also influenced by the previous two factors. If either of the first two is impaired they will almost certainly shorten the potential degree of personal development.

In the next chapter we will look at some of the ways these developmental kinks can manifest.

Chapter Six
State Properties

In this chapter and the next we look the properties of states and the human personality. While these chapters are neither exhaustive nor conclusive, they describe a general theoretical structure of the personality. Many statements may be presented as though they were facts but they are only within the context of the theory.

The structure of the personality is the result of interaction among the cognitive, perceptual, and developmental processes we discussed in the previous chapters. In this chapter we will find out what happens when life goes well during our developmental years and we will describe what happens when we experience emotional trauma along our path of development.

From the position of our original makeup, we possess full flexibility to occupy and operate from any of the 500-plus states of being. Some states or meta-states require age-related cognitive skills to utilize. But we don't hold any state as off-limits. The result is that people easily utilize states in the midrange—equilibrium states—because these states usually work most effectively, by creating the desired outcome with a minimum amount of unwanted consequence.

While I don't believe that we start our lives as a *tabula rasa*, I do believe we are born in an unencumbered, intact condition. The equilibrium theory holds that people begin as essentially whole beings who possess the full complement of states, even though our cognitive development limits access to higher states early in life. The idea that we begin as a whole, intact being is similar to the theories of Carl Rogers and Carl Jung. While we lack full development at birth, we possess the essential ingredients to fully develop. Rogers (1961) states that we begin much like an acorn that evolves into an oak tree. Unless circumstances interfere, we develop fully. Jung (1953) asserts in his theory of personality that we innately possess all features of the human personality such as good and evil. Our task over our lifespan is integrating our features into a conscious and unconscious whole. In the theory presented within this book, I suggest that we do possess all features of the human personality and that we will utilize them freely unless some emotional trauma occurs during the use of a particular state. If an emotional trauma occurs during the use of a state, we then disown the state, displacing our self from equilibrium. At the start of life we have no reason not to allow total freedom to our self.

Fragmenting of self and the limitations that follow happens only as a defense mechanism to preserve the organism.

Our personality may also include, as part of its original makeup, certain basic response styles. People seem to respond to adversity in one of two ways: they either turn up their behavior, increasing their current behavioral style, or turn down their behavior. People also seem either to give or take as a means of satisfying their personal needs. These two categories of styles may dovetail at times. As an example, let us look at what goes on in the early stages of an interpersonal relationship.

In these early stages, each person continues behaving as when they first met. The relationship carries on because of the way each person acts. But, when a conflict comes up between the two, things may change. One or both of the people in the relationship may feel threatened or insecure. As a result, one person may turn down their assertive behavior by becoming more passive. The other person may turn up their behavior by becoming more assertive or even aggressive. The now passive person may make peace offerings and attempt giving to the other person to satisfy the other's needs. The giving one tries to verify the stability of the relationship by giving more of themselves.

The now increasingly assertive person uses the taking strategy to get needs met. This person may be more demanding of the partner, may try to verify the stability of the relationship by finding out how much and how often the other can give. The aggressive taker in the relationship may be saying, "I need from you, give to me," while the passive other is saying, "Here, take from me, let me give to you." Not only does each person lose equilibrium in this process, but the relationship becomes unbalanced, losing *its* equilibrium as well.

People seem to use one of these two strategies as coping mechanisms when their natural equilibrium state meets adversity. They do this rather than do more of what was working to get the relationship going well in the first place. They assume the state was the cause of the adversity (transductive logic).

When things go wrong in life, people tend to revert to old coping strategies.

Now let's come back to more of a general overview of this theory's view of human nature. If nothing interferes with our nature, we begin with a structure of personality similar to X and Y axes (see Figure 6.1). The X axis extends in a horizontal line and consists of primary states, what you think about information received through your physical senses. The Y axis extends vertically from the X axis consisting of meta-states.

The closer to the center of the X axis, the larger the cluster of equilibrium states, just waiting for you to use them effectively. The states of disequilibrium reside away from the center. The further the utilized state is away from the center, the more frustrating the results tend to be.

Now this is not to say there are not exceptions to the general rule that states of equilibrium make for the most effective outcomes. If someone breaks into your house, you may need to be extremely aggressive to defend and protect yourself. But this provides a good example of a principle about states, a meta-principle if you will: the further away from equilibrium, the more the states are used in defense of self.

This defense can be of physical as well as emotional self. It also seems true to say that the further away from equilibrium, the lower, or more primitive, the developmental level of operation. Remember Loevinger's level of development called "self-protective"? This stage of development is displayed by the states that are away from the center. The developmental level that Loevinger called "impulsive" contains the states furthest from equilibrium

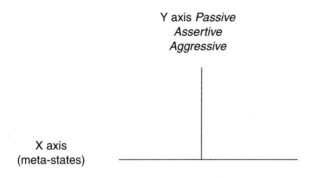

Y axis *Passive*
Assertive
Aggressive

X axis
(meta-states)

Figure 6.1: Axes of states – primary and meta

on the X axis. At the impulsive level of development the person actually believes that he is the emotion or state. He does not just experience the state: it becomes or consumes him and he lives at the affect of the state. This seems to hold true for either extreme of disequilibrium, with aggression and passivity serving in this example.

Two further principles about states bear mentioning here. There is a direct correlation between the distance the state is from equilibrium and the degree of awareness and egocentrism. The further away from equilibrium the state in operation, the narrower is the awareness of information in the environment. The second principle is that the state will become more egocentric, or defensive. For example, the more extreme the passivity or aggression, the less the person will notice the big picture. Foresight, patience, and flexibility go out the window at the extremes of the continuum.

The Piaget concepts of *centering* come into play here. Centering limits awareness and actually begets more extreme perceptions that encourage more extreme response states. Once a person centers, then the only way to explain what happens in the field of awareness is to use the information present in the limited tunnel of awareness. Also, notice that the more extreme the state, the more it represents a defense or self-protective mechanism, made up of egocentric ways. This process leads to other cognitive errors such as *transductive logic* (supposed cause and effect must exist within the narrow field of awareness, since that is all the information with which to work) and the other categories of restricted thought that Piaget named.

Continuum state variations

At any point along the continuum of primary states (such as assertiveness) you can find variations. The primary states may range from a total absence of assertiveness, through passivity to an extreme degree of assertiveness known as aggression. Now each of these primary states at any point along the horizontal axis can have a meta-state about it. Each individual state of equilibrium, such as assertiveness, can also be conceived as having a state on the Y axis—Meta-States^R. Hall identifies these as thoughts *about* thoughts or states *about* states (1995). Along the X continuum, we can find a region of a constructive midrange for any one particular state.

As an example of the axis structure of states, let's use the resource state known as assertiveness. This particular state exists as a primary or meta-state because you can apply it to other states and assertively, passively, or aggressively express your state of self-doubt or confidence, for example. But the point is that state of assertiveness serves as a good example of equilibrium, with the states of passivity and aggression representing disequilibrium. The meta-state "assertiveness" serves as a vehicle for self-expression. We can display any state, primary or meta, in an assertive, passive, or aggressive manner. Assertiveness and its variations act as *state modifiers*.

The assertive canal

As a metaphor, we might imagine assertive functioning as a canal channeling the flow of self-expression out through the mouth and into the larger environment. If obstacles block the flow, then expression diverts to one side or the other, making for passivity or aggression. The blocking or damming stems from a SEE and a resulting limiting belief about the future use of that state. Navigating straight out the central canal may endanger the ship, or state, on its journey toward the mouth of the river. The aggressive form of self-expression might be thought of as rapids. Believing the straight-flowing assertiveness river is blocked, the flow speeds up so as to ride over the dam with enough power to force the self-expression out, but in an unregulated manner.

It seems reasonable to say that symptoms manifest in the form of either passive or aggressive expressions of states of equilibrium.

Whichever the scenario, a person believes he cannot assertively express the particular state of equilibrium. The result is that he either overexpresses or underexpresses for the situation.

Restoring assertiveness skills alone, though, will not provide a solution. Teaching a person on the ground how to pack a parachute and pull the ripcord will not overcome her fear of heights. The absence of a skill, assertiveness, was not the reason she was passive in the first place. Rather, the person feared assertively expressing herself. A part of that person will still object to utilizing the feared state in spite of knowing how to use it. Fear serves as meta to assertiveness and so fear rules.

The original factor that motivated the diversion from equilibrium still exists. The skill of assertiveness does not have enough power to override the previously existing belief about the danger of asserting self. For example, some clients that I have worked with possess a strong fear of conflict. No amount of assertiveness training will remove that fear and lead to a state of comfort with conflict. The solution comes from finding out which cognitive errors led to the fear, or which Piagetian thought categories are in play. You can also identify which developmental level the fear of conflict stems from (conformist, most likely) and help the perspective to evolve to a developmentally higher level, rising above the limitations.

Whether therapy addresses the thoughts or the developmental level of the person, many intervention techniques exist. These can bring the client from discomfort with conflict to comfort, utilizing the state of assertiveness. In the process of therapy she finds and becomes comfortable utilizing a long-abandoned state that allows her to develop and use conflict-resolution skills. The client does not make the skill her own.

When just the skills of assertiveness are taught, without developing comfort with the state, the state exists dissociated from the person.

At the midrange of states, people think, feel, and behave in a manner that respects their own rights, while at the same time respecting the rights of others. The state of assertiveness permits flexible negotiating between parties while working within a framework of mutual respect. Such people actively, yet respectfully, pursue the outcome they desire. If the state extends further to the right along the X axis, it eventually extends outside the midrange and becomes aggression. This state contains thoughts, feelings, and behaviors that operate respectfully toward self but are not respecting of others' rights.

Aggression limits available solutions because it excludes others from consideration or respect. If, however, the chosen operating position of the state moves enough to the left of center, it will again move outside the midrange. When the operating position moves too far left, it then becomes passivity. This state includes thoughts, feelings, and behaviors that operate without respecting self, but place sole emphasis on respecting the rights of others. This position of passivity also limits potential solutions as it too disregards one party's rights. In this case, self is excluded.

The state imbalance sets in motion a series of compensating mechanisms much like the aftereffect of a stone landing in a still pond.

Disequilibrium occurs at either range outside the midpoint spread and the ripples go on to affect many thoughts and behaviors in a broad range of areas. When the disequilibrium-based response happens, it will only lead to additional issues that will need tending. In other words, occupying and operating any state other than the vacated equilibrium state creates more problems.

Both aggression and passivity create fallout. When a person behaves aggressively he usually has relationship damage to repair. When behaving passively he usually has damage to repair from not upholding personal boundaries. Only the midpoint state of assertiveness cleanly resolves issues.

The solution process involves returning to the state midrange. One way to help a person return to the midpoint is to cite counterexamples to the fear that blocks the midpoint state (for details see 'The difference is the difference' in Chapter Eleven). A person can also go to a "meta" position where he can clear the perception hurdles that block access to midpoints. We will look closely at these methods in the last chapter. Perceptual hurdles, in this case, consist of perceiving crucial events in the past as endangering free access of the midrange-state.

The person in the midst of a problem state sees present situations through the past and responds in childlike ways, owing to childlike perception. As we saw earlier, when a traumatic event happens while a person is associated into a particular state, the individual then decides this state is off-limits. In essence the person declares the state unsafe and vacates it as though it were a condemned and dangerous building.

Two universal behavioral principles

In the process of observing myself, clients with whom I work, and general human behavior, I noticed what appeared to be two universal truths about human behavior that I believe people operate from:

- If some is good, more is better.
- People will change always and only for a higher meta-level of functioning.

Every behavioral style we use is in place for the simple reason that it works, or at least it used to work, or we believe it will work now. Some would argue, rightly, that not all behaviors bring effective results. But what causes the chosen behaviors to be used even though they do not work effectively now? The belief that chosen behaviors sometimes do not work is true if you look only at the surface. Often the surface goal is measured externally, such as winning a race, racking up great sales, or achieving promotion at work. But a deeper internal goal may be very different, such as to feel peaceful or content.

People sometimes sabotage their own efforts at reaching their declared goals. This sabotage is a sure sign of conflict between goals at the surface and goals at deeper levels. There is a crucial point here: beliefs play a moderating role in this conflict between surface goals and deeper goals.

Case study
Let's take the case of Julie, a woman in her early thirties who came to me for counseling. She came primarily because she was not yet married with children. While discussing this issue, she brought up another concern. Julie made a good salary of around $90,000 per year. But she made no effort to save any money. She had no funds set up for retirement. Her checking account continued to accumulate huge balances. She claimed she really wanted to change this but could not get herself to consult a financial adviser who could set up a retirement plan. A surface goal of saving money was consistently avoided. "It's so frustrating," Julie said. "I want to be financially secure but I just can't get myself to do anything about it."

Once we looked beneath the surface we found an interesting belief interacting with a state she was striving to reach. She believed that if she set up and used a retirement plan it would mean that she would remain forever single. She would have accepted her single status as permanent and just moved on with life. Her bigger goal (meta-level) of getting married and having children was designed to bring fulfillment. To Julie, the two goals seemed at odds.

The belief Julie held about saving money and the fulfillment she anticipated from having a family prevented her from saving money. Julie saw these two goals as mutually exclusive (either/or thinking). After she had cleared up the tangle by clarifying the two goals, a new belief formed and she could begin saving money toward retirement. Julie came to realize that by saving money she could actually enhance her eventual marriage and family life. Now the two goals could coexist.

The general conflict between conscious and unconscious goals is very often the reason a person comes in for counseling. Clients seek alignment between their conscious and unconscious minds at the highest meta-level, not just at the level of conflict. This alignment breeds consistency between beliefs and behaviors. As Bateson (1972) stated, the higher-level states, when activated, rule over the lower-level states. Sometimes therapy is ineffective because it addresses only the surface without accessing and aligning the higher levels of thought, development, and beliefs.

Sometimes therapy is ineffective because it addresses only the surface without accessing and aligning the higher levels of thought, development, and beliefs.

Very often a person has mixed feelings and mixed goals such that the unconscious goal—in the above case marriage and family— wins out, while the conscious goal of retirement savings is not reached. This makes it look as if the behavioral strategy of not setting up a retirement fund did not work. But the strategy worked perfectly for the unconscious goal. It works, I suspect, whether it is for the conscious or unconscious, to provide support and protection for a meta-state.

In the case just described, saving money endangered the state of fulfillment. At least this was held as true in the old belief system. The principle here is that behavior is purposeful and is designed to satisfy or protect a state or meta-state. And, when the decision is one of protecting either a state or a meta-state, the meta-state always wins. An unconscious goal holds the upper hand and dominates over a conscious goal.

Now to the first of the universal principles we met earlier: "If some is good, more is better." If the behavioral style becomes ineffective after initial success at sustaining or defending its boss, the meta-state, it has only a few options. If at first you don't succeed, try, try again. This age-old adage sets the tone for the usual first response in the face of less than effective strategies. If something doesn't work, but it *used to* work (the crucial determining factor) we almost always just try it harder, to try to make the once successful method succeed again As we know, this only deepens the "problem" and the vicious circle begins.

Consider the agoraphobic as an example. She first restricts herself from going to places where she's had a panic attack. She sees the place where she had an attack as having power to evoke one (transductive logic). If narrowing her world and limiting her environmental contact doesn't relieve panic and anxiety, she will tighten her circle even more. The process can continue until the individual becomes housebound. This general principle holds for all "symptoms", be they anxiety, overeating, paranoia, or depression. And this principle is what gets us into trouble. However, it is also this very same process, when applied to a different goal, that gets us *out* of trouble. The odd factor here is that the person focuses on what *used* to work rather than what is happening *now* (ineffective results). Doing more of what does not work now only brings more frustration.

First-order change means that, when a person meets with frustration, he only does more of the behavior that is already in action.

The first principle mentioned here is similar to the concept of first- and second-order change identified by Watzlawick *et al.* (1974). The belief is that if it worked once it just needs to be done again but with more fervor. Second-order change means that the person changes the process of his behavior.

Second-order change involves applying a different process to solve the problem.

Imagine that you walk up to your friend's house and knock on the door. You know he is home but he doesn't come to the door, so you knock again. This used to get him to answer the door so surely it will again. After getting no answer this time, you decide that you really need to knock more forcefully. This brings no response either. Now, motivated by sore knuckles, second-order change takes charge. You decide to go around to the back yard of your friend's house and there is your friend.

Now let us look at the second principle: "People will change always and only for a higher meta-level of functioning." People change for something better than what they already possess. There would be no point or motivation in changing for an equal status. By "possess", I do include material goods. But at a deeper, more influential level I mean people change if the new choice lets them adhere to their higher values, which in turn lets them experience a higher meta-state. People don't change for no reason. Through this living of their higher values they then come to experience a higher level of meta-state. Thus people will change always and only for a higher level of meta-state functioning.

The concept and act of charity will provide us with a good example of how we change for a higher-level value and experience a higher meta-state. While charity also includes forgiveness, here we'll refer to charity as the act of giving something of your time, energy, or material goods to another person. During the act of charity we give up something that we value. We do this because we decide that someone else has a greater need, and acknowledging and acting upon that need allows us to fulfill a higher value and then experience a higher meta-state.

In NLP, the six-step reframe is also an example of changing for a higher meta-state. In this six-step reframe developed by Connirae Andreas, the goal is to elicit from the client the highest known purpose behind a behavior. By letting the higher purpose guide behavior, the client can find more flexible and resourceful methods to fulfill the goal rather than experience a rigid sticking point at lower levels of thought and behavior. You may say that the reframe works by citing a higher purpose in order to motivate a person to change. But above and more powerful than the purpose is the state the person comes to experience as a result of fulfilling the higher purpose. States drive behavior.

Let's look at how the two principles work together to bring about constructive outcomes. The "more is better" that got us into trouble gets us out of trouble when applied to the second principle. By applying the more-is-better approach to meta-levels of thought, we end up with more meta-state-based choices instead of more and limiting primary-state choices.

Case study

Earlier, I described working with a client who did not trust her own judgment. She used to trust others but, after a series of relationships in which she found ways to get taken advantage of, she reached a point of no longer trusting anyone. I received confirmation from her that she did not trust people. We then proceeded to note how she mistrusted her trusting—did not trust her own ability to trust.

At this point I expressed amazement at how she found a way of trusting her mistrust of trust each and every time. That is quite a consistent level of trust. So we found a well-developed and effective ability to trust. It just existed well below the supposed protective surface. These levels of thought, feeling, and process correlate to those levels of thought Hall (1995, 2000) refers to as meta-levels of being. Meta-stating, a client relies on these levels of the states.

This client would not easily change her behavior at the level of the problem, not trusting, and just begin selectively trusting others. How could she feel safe doing this? This change would be merely an even trade of stopping old behavior and starting new behavior without strengthening her sense of emotional safety. There was not enough incentive to shift. This would happen only after a lengthy and arduous task of developing skills within that level of functioning. This almost certainly would bring about some fear-based "resistance" on her part.

This would come about because, if she just started trusting people, she would feel vulnerable and her self-protection would kick in to protect her from potential harm. A whole lot of convincing would need to happen for her to let go of her defenses. Eventually, after enough counterexamples, suggesting which types and degrees of trust are safe, she would combine these new learnings into a new belief and behavior. New beliefs about self and others would then form. But this path seems the slow way for elevating the client to levels that exist meta to their symptomatic level. As you may recall, Einstein stated that the solution to problems exists on thought levels above the problem level. I will add that there is no solution within the problem, so don't look there for one.

> **There is no solution within the problem, so don't look there for one.**

From the point of accessing her genuine ability to trust her internal process, we identified both the emotional state and kinesthetic sensations for this state of trust. Once she did this she rediscovered a forgotten ability of experiencing a "gut feeling" about situations and people. She had actually stopped trusting herself. But her gut instincts had never let her down. Her gut always "felt" accurately. We continued dusting off this state, identifying its many attributes and identifying applications in the present and future as a guiding force so she could feel safe. By this time she associated into this "trust of self" state and eagerly began applying it to her life.

This whole therapeutic process took place over five sessions. At last contact, about two months later, she reported feeling great and continued operating effectively from her state of self-trust. Why wouldn't she? She experienced more of what she really wanted to experience. If some is good, more is better. She changed only because she could experience a higher level, meta-level, of functioning—anything less would not do.

> **Once a person experiences a higher level of functioning, she will voluntarily release the problematic level.**

By utilizing the apparently inherent human structure that includes levels of abstraction (Korzybski, 1933, 1994), we can more-quickly find and utilize solutions to ineffective behavioral styles. Once a person experiences a higher-level meta-state and the higher functioning this state this brings, she will voluntarily release the problematic level. She realizes more of what she really wants. Seeing herself successfully enacting the new beliefs and behaviors in the future provides a more complete "tamping down" into the desired state. It lets her experience the "if some is good, more is better" principle by imaging how well it will work to provide the desired outcome.

Now we hook this first principle (more is better) to the second principle, which says that people will change always and only for a higher meta-level of functioning. The very process once getting us into trouble now gets us out of trouble and maintains the new level. If we make the "more" in "more is better" comprise a higher meta-state, then we get more of what we want in and from our self.

All effective therapy seems to operate by utilizing these two principles. Cognitive, behavioral, gestalt, Rogerian, NLP, or any other style of therapy strives to lift the client to a higher level of meta operations. And this higher meta-level also corresponds to a higher developmental level. Symptoms represent nothing other than misguided efforts to reach higher Meta-States[R] of functioning. Assisting clients in accessing and operating higher resourceful Meta-States[R] allows the change process to begin. Once he has reached the more effective meta-state, the client will naturally operate the first principle to maintain himself at the new desirable level.

We have covered quite a lot in this chapter, so let us end with a summary:

- States exist on a continuum. The center third consists of equilibrium states while the thirds on either side of center consist of states of disequilibrium.
- In response to adverse events, people either increase or decrease the state. For example, assertiveness may become aggression or passivity.
- Not all states of equilibrium are functional and not all disequilibrium states are dysfunctional. The difference is whether or not a person returns to equilibrium states after a necessary use of a disequilibrium state.
- The further away from equilibrium the state used, the more the state is in defense of self and the more egocentric the state.
- If some is good, more is better. When a formerly effective state no longer brings about a desired outcome we will amplify or intensify that state as our first response to feeling frustrated.

- People will always and only change for a higher meta-level of functioning. They will not just trade one behavior or state for another. The change must bring about a state that ranks higher on the feel-good scale than the current state.

Chapter Seven
The Dynamics of Interacting States

While the two universal behavioral principles demonstrate themselves through the client example we saw in the last chapter, another principle about states now becomes evident. We could divide up states, whether primary or meta, into (a) those that actively propel a person toward engaging the environment and (b) those that act passively or disengage the person from the environment. One of the very first behaviors an infant learns is pulling an object closer or pushing it away (Flavell, 1963).

We could divide up states into those that actively propel a person toward engaging the environment and those that disengage the person from the environment.

This early skill of pushing and pulling then lives out in our relationship with our states. A person can pull a state toward himself and utilize it or he can push it away and disconnect from it. He can also pull himself in closer to the environment to engage more fully or push the environment away and disengage. The relationship in this case exists between individual states or the state and the environment. While all states do not necessarily fit into the positive and negative categories, many do display this principle of moving us toward or away from other states or the environment.

We might refer them as positive and negative, respectively. This is not a value statement, and these positive and negative states are not necessarily effective or ineffective. Rather, "positive" and "negative" refer to the properties of the states—how they interact with the other states or the environment. If you experience the positive state of joy, you generally move toward the environment or welcome another state about which you feel joyous. You may feel joyous about your new job or your ability to experience the state of love. Notice how this state of joy moves you to engage the environment or other state.

Negative states such as dislike tend to move a person away from another state or the environmental circumstance. Another negative state, indifference, tends at least to disengage a person from a state or the environment.

Let us use the state of "indifference" as an example of a state that is negative. In some situations it is useful to be indifferent. We may do well to act indifferently about snide remarks from others. We may do well to utilize the state of indifference to block out things around us that could distract us from reaching a goal. On the other hand, if you are married, you would not do yourself a favor by reacting with indifference about your wedding anniversary. The state of attending to this situation will help keep you in good graces and give you an opportunity to express your deepest feeling toward your loved one.

States such as resistance, contemplation, rebelliousness, thoughtfulness, docility, mistrust, worthlessness, being withdrawn, uncertainty, rejection, and doubt qualify as negative states. These states prevent us from engaging and utilizing other states such as when you doubt your confidence. And these negative states put our direct interaction with the environment on hold such as when you withhold your approval. They provide a distancing or buffer between self and the environment. Many other states fit this criterion as well. You can apply the principles of the definition for determining which other states qualify.

It is significant that negative states require a positive state behind them to provide support in order to manifest the positive intent behind all behavior. Negative states remain dormant unless activated by positive states. One must move toward an away-from strategy in order for it to become actively applied. Negative states cannot function independently. The positive state must remain the force behind the negative state for as long as it remains active. It was trust in the case of the woman who mistrusted others. She had to trust (positive state) her mistrust (negative state) to be able to mistrust others.

Doing the maths

You may think of the relationship between positive and negative states as being like that of positive and negative numbers. When multiplying two positives the result is a positive. Multiplying a negative by a positive state results in a negative state. Two negatives multiplied together create a positive.

The formula where a negative state is engaged or multiplied by another negative state plays out in the linguistic process known as "apply to self" (Hall and Bodenhamer, 1997). This technique applies a negative state to itself, another negative state, and they cancel each out, leaving the original positive state of equilibrium present. For example, when we feel bored with boredom we return to a state of interest in finding stimulation.

As another example, in order for doubt to be utilized we must believe our doubt. The positive state, belief, gives life to the negative state of doubt. We can sustain our doubt only as long as we believe it. This state of doubt may apply to something we perceive in our environment or to another state within us. When we doubt our doubt it no longer exists. While degrees of doubt exist and some people achieve a terminal degree in doubt, the more doubt is applied to the existing doubt the more it diminishes. What do we then experience? Perhaps certainty, confidence, or trust takes the place of doubt.

Conversely, applying a negative state to a positive state will create a negative state. Maybe you doubt your trust. But to do this you have to trust (positive) your doubt (negative) of your trust (positive). You have a positive state propelling a negative state, which is applied to a positive state. This is a kind of state sandwich. It seems to be the inherent structure state dynamics.

The crucial factor here is that for any negative state to become activated a positive state is required.

The "apply to self" reframe provides a very effective change technique. I would also suggest directly accessing the positive state of *trust* of doubt for more leverage and future use. Once you contact the positive state and associate the client into it, meta-state this state.

The positive always exists behind or underneath the negative as the driver. The negative state serves only as a shield for protecting the original positive state. Freeing the positive resource involves accessing and associating into the positive. This allows a person to apply the resource state directly to the environment while inevitably imagining the desired outcome. Previously, the original positive state was associated with the past SEE every time the person thought about using the state in the present.

The process of meta-stating begins with a positive state but adds higher consciousness to it, making it a much stronger state. This stronger state is then up to the task at hand. Upon meta-stating the original state, the person can see the present and future in an updated version rather than use the past as a reference. Once she experiences this new consciousness, she finds that anything less is undesirable. If some is good, more is better, and people will always and only change for a higher meta-level of functioning.

As another example of a negative state applied to another negative state, consider someone who withdraws from her environment. In order to withdraw she has to engage the state of withdrawing. If she withdraws her withdrawing she returns to the original state of equilibrium. In this case, a state like "engaging" or "reaching out" to the environment comes forth. She is now free to engage her environment. The original resource state empowers her to express herself in the larger external environment. The process of meta-stating promotes further development of the original resource state by enhancing its abilities with additional foresight, flexibility, and patience. Meta-stating invokes the advanced resources associated with higher human development.

The levels of human development inversely correlate with the degree to which a person protects and pursues her own needs.

The higher the level of development, the less self-absorbed the person. When acting in altruistic ways toward universal needs, rather than just her own needs, she functions from higher levels of development. The firefighter putting out a house fire concerns herself less with her own needs and more with the needs of others.

In the process of tending another's needs, she also coincidentally meets her own higher-order needs. Further, more evolved states possess broader awareness that allows for a feeling of safety. The environment no longer dictates to or endangers states when someone is perceiving from higher levels of development. The individual realizes that only she can choose to utilize or disengage from a state. The result is safe expression of states of equilibrium.

The same structure of states holds true for layers of Meta-States[R] above a primary state. To identify the positive state, find the highest-level negative meta-state. The next step involves identifying and then accessing the positive meta-state that operates the "protective" negative. One always presents itself. For example, in order to display the state of "anxiety" you must employ the meta-state of comfort. We apply comfort to anxiety for activating it.

Can a person feel anxious about feeling anxious? Yes and no. A person can choose to feel anxious about feeling anxious. This anxiety about anxiety moves a person into a heightened state of fear or maybe even panic. But, before the anxiety about anxiety could be activated, he must decide at some level that it feels most comfortable to feel anxious about feeling anxious. Of course, this does not work, and the strategy produces only panic. But the state of comfort gives the go-ahead for activating anxiety about anxiety. The design feels the safest as a defense against anxiety. At some level the person experiencing anxiety decided that this state, anxiety, was the most comfortable option known.

When a person is in the midst of experiencing anxiety he will report that he feels more vulnerable without his anxiety and, oddly, more comfortable with his anxiety. Yes, this person's conscious mind will tell you that he hates his anxiety. But once you probe his unconscious mind you will find that this same person is reluctant to release his anxiety, lest he feel uncomfortable or unsafe. His anxiety has become a comfort to him in a very convoluted way. At the deepest level of dysfunction a person feels afraid not to feel afraid. It is the last bastion of defense, against fear of all things!

Maladaptive states, or disequilibrium states, possess a state of equilibrium as a driving force. When a person operates from a disequilibrium state, she often reports feeling as though a desired state were missing from within. We do not need to look for the missing state. It is not really missing, but resides as the power behind the throne. Associating into "depression" requires our associating into the meta-state known as hope.

Oddly, the depressed person hoped that some disconnection from a state—joy, for instance—would solve some problem. She then disowns joy in search of a solution state within herself. Not initially finding the solution, the depressed person just goes deeper into herself to find the solution. The solution is not elsewhere within, since joy was not the problem, but she just dives that much deeper into herself, accumulating limiting states and deeper depression along the way.

Case study
I'll give you an example of a client I worked with. Dave was raised by his chronically depressed mother, who chose depression as a method of controlling her life and the behavior of her children. When Dave acted depressed, his mother rewarded this behavior by consoling him and giving support. But if Dave shifted to acting happy she took his shift as a display of strength that would surely move him away from her clutches. She responded to Dave's happiness by withdrawing her support and increasing her symptoms of "depression". As a child he saw little choice but to abandon his happiness in favor of mother's approval.

Now an adult, Dave could not allow himself to sustain any degree of happiness for fear of his mother's rejection. She still pulled this emotional manipulation in his adulthood. Feeling the absence of happiness in his life, he then went on a prolonged but futile search within in order to find out how he could respond differently, how he could turn the depression around. He would search within and only feel more lost and depressed because he could not find the answer. He did not know he was at the affect of his mother's manipulation, which caused him to abandon his own happiness.

He continued believing he was doing something wrong in life and blamed himself, developing a stronger sense of incompetence. All the while he needed only to reclaim and utilize his state of happiness. But he could not realize this until the veil was lifted from his mother's dynamics and agenda. It required many years during his childhood to move from a natural state of happiness to abandoning the state, becoming depressed and forming limiting beliefs about self.

A natural chronological order exists within the layering of states. The surface state exists as the most recent addition to the state beneath it.

The dynamics described above reveal another principle about states. Backtracking through states is like an archeological dig. Simply look for the deepest equilibrium state of the dysfunctional primary or meta-state. That state is the one the client desires to access but has cloaked in a maladaptive state. Upon accessing this equilibrium state, invite the person to associate into the resource state, meta-state, this and then re-examine the situation and future-pace.

Hall and Bodenhamer (1997) draw on this natural chronological structure of states in a particular intervention they developed. The backtracking method simply retraces the states utilized from the most recent problematic state back to the original resource state—an equilibrium state. Once again, the equilibrium state is not the problem: the person just thought it was due to transductive logic at the time of a traumatic event. In Dave's case, the state of happiness was punished while depression was rewarded, so he chose to utilize the state of depression.

The structure of a maladaptive mental pattern includes several layers. The outermost part consists of the state causing distress. In the case of the mistrusting person it is the mistrust. However, we can safely presuppose the negative state is actually put on top of an original resource state. This results in the mistrust of the person's original trust. Now comes the third layer, and the most tricky to grasp. We back up to before she mistrusts her trust and find the next layer. This consists of her trust of her mistrust of her trust. If she did not trust her mistrust of her trust she could not activate this elaborate dysfunctional system. Her trust gives it life. This last layer consists of the original core state, operating from the point of equilibrium. Essentially, each maladaptive state becomes a sandwich with resource states as the bread.

By performing this state backtracking, we utilize a "meta-timeline" of sorts. We go back in "meta-time" to the original unfettered equilibrium state and operate from it.

Having identified the core state, the person then associates into it. She then uses this state as the platform for reviewing the situation and applying the state directly to the issue. By performing this state backtracking, we utilize a "meta-timeline" of sorts. This meta-timeline consists of a time-ordered sequence of states and meta-states the person experienced in response to an event, and the responses to the responses (the meta-states). We go back in "meta-time" to the original unfettered equilibrium state and operate from it. This general structure seems to be always present in people. When encountering dysfunction, you can usually assume resource states reside on each side of the nonresource state, supporting it and giving life to the negative state.

Many examples exist of positive states behind a negative one. You can begin to think up these yourself. As an example of the three layers of states in maladaptive schemes, think about a person who backs away from others because of his shyness. We then suppose the person actually backs away from the state of engaging others. However, he also engages backing away from engaging. The state of engaging then functions as the state of equilibrium. The person associates into this state of engaging and uses it as the resource state for dealing with others. The once shy person now fulfills his desired outcome. We can count on finding the original state intact but likely operating from off-center, meaning that he turned down the degree of engaging on the continuum to such a degree that it/he became silent.

To activate the state of depression, a person must first associate into a state of hope. The depressed person hopes that depression will lead to a desired outcome.

Let's use depression as another for instance so you can notice the dynamics at work. The result is feeling hopeful about depressing hope as a solution. For a person displaying the state of "fear" she must be "comfortable" with being afraid. We could also safely state the person doing "fear" must fear comfort so she added a protective layer. This ever-present arrangement apparently applies to all maladaptive states. Disequilibrium provides another way of defining the maladaptive states. They operate off-center, limiting our response repertoire. This results in an unbalanced life both internally and externally.

The middle layer, which essentially negates the original state by modifying it, is an initial defense mechanism. The negative state seems to occur in response to circumstances that people perceive as threatening. They then abandon the current state and adapt the alternative strategy as a basic survival mechanism.

You may think of the negative state engaged by the positive state as acting like a protective coating. The individual does not believe the positive state is strong enough for the situation, thus endangered. But these negative, supposedly protective, states operate from a limited perception and, as a result, limit response options. The only effective solution is to raise the consciousness of the original positive state.

To protect the positive state, a negative shell is placed over the positive state. The person then engages the environment from this supposedly safer position.

Consider a workaholic. This person once operated from a state that might be called "productivity" or "achievement". She believed behaving this way equated to feeling competent. However, at some point, while she was operating from that state, something happened that she perceived as threatening. Maybe a communication from a significant other led to her feeling that any achievement is never enough, that she must always strive for more. This conclusion may have resulted from spotty and fleeting approval from this significant other. Right when she might have experienced a sense of accomplishment or contentment, the perceived approval is withdrawn. Now she must start all over again to regain this significant other's approval, making the state of contentment a dangerous state because contentment comes to be equated with the removal of approval.

She thus abandons the state of contentment, choosing one of two responses. She may turn up that achievement-oriented behavior, making for more time and energy spent in producing more output. In essence she redefines the criteria to experience contentment to a higher level of work and productivity. Anything less than the new and intensified level is now labeled discontent (if some is good, more is better). The state of discontent may easily lead her to question her competence, since she'll use egocentricity to blame herself for not achieving a state of contentment. She now feels incompetent about her competency.

She then chases the state of contentment and competence, but, just as tomorrow never comes, the state remains elusive. This never-ending chase is also the result of her basing the sense of contentment and competence on actions and not on just being aware of the complement of internal resources that naturally make her permanently competent. For the workaholic, the source of competence or contentment is believed to reside outside the individual and so is in almost constant need of replenishing. You may be able to take in the experience of competence after a successful act, but, if you do not have a place for it to roost within you, the experience of competence will be temporary, setting up the drive to experience competence again and again.

This sort of chase for the state of contentment opens up to infinity. There is always more to accomplish and the task is never completed.

Realize that the core of this endless chase originates from the belief that the state of contentment exists externally to the individual. Lower levels of development attribute states to the environment, setting up endless chases and adversarial relationships. Once we realize that the state of contentment, and all states, exist within, then we can freely access and experience them at will.

Reacting to the belief that the state of contentment is external to her, the person now seeks but avoids the state. If she accomplishes something she starts feeling content, but must immediately vacate this state because of its past unpleasant implications (loss of approval from a significant other). Contentment now equates with complacency, laziness, or a similar state. How else could she interpret the circumstances as long as external consequences determine the value of her states?

She continues seeking accomplishments that she craves, but, upon feeling content about a job well done, she must immediately pursue another task. This exhausting cycle comes from the state arrangement of contentment about discontentment about contentment. She simply must utilize the state of contentment about something (Maslow's "We must be who we are"), so she applies it to discontentment rather than to a task accomplished. The resource needed for her to experience utter fulfillment remains in perfect condition, but she just aims it at a target that is causing discontent. In other words, she can and must feel contentment, but she just settles for feeling content about feeling discontentment toward her contentment.

This process of state layers came into play with a client who could not allow herself to feel good about any of her many accomplishments. She felt compelled to feel bad about feeling good. At this point I suggested that she must then be able to feel very good about her strategy of feeling bad about feeling good! The worse she felt about feeling good the better she could feel! She realized how ridiculous her logic was and stopped it. Through what past lens must she be viewing the present and future? The past is a poor lens through which to view anything other than former strategies that successfully led to desired outcomes. The present lends itself to accurate viewing of the present and the future lends itself wonderfully to planning the best use of our present to create a rewarding future.

Bipolarizing states

As we have seen, two response styles exist when we feel that the original equilibrium state is unavailable. There is the one option of turning up the efforts to achieve success. The other response style involves turning down the level of time and energy, bringing a decrease in productivity. This method comes into effect in an effort to avoid further criticism or sense of failure. The belief here is: "If I put forth less effort, I will expose myself for criticism less. If I expose myself less, there will be less risk of potential disapproval. If you can't see, hear, or generally detect my efforts there will be nothing specific to draw criticism."

While responding to the blockage of contentment in a manner opposite to that of the workaholic, this person shares a common concern with her. He, too, feels incompetent about competence. Taking the process of self-constricting to an extreme may explain what ends up being diagnosed as a schizoid personality. In this syndrome, the person maintains a flat affect, showing no interest or significant action in any facet of life. Instead of overdoing, he prefers to disengage from life, perhaps as a safety mechanism.

Choosing either direction as compensation only leads to a spiraling process of further disequilibrium. Any mistake that draws criticism after the initial adjustment leads to further moves away from the original state of equilibrium. This person moves toward either end on the competence continuum, becoming a whirling dervish on the way to burnout or a person who gradually shrinks his world until it comes to a virtual standstill.

Moving away from any of the equilibrium states makes bipolar beings of us all. We then occupy either end of the poles, moving from one to the other.

In fact it is not unusual for a person to move from one end of the continuum to the other. Witness the person who seems to go in fits of productivity, spending himself into exhaustion and not working again for some time. This is not a chemical imbalance. He just unfortunately believes the equilibrium state, something like contentment, to be off-limits. While chemical imbalances do eventually come to exist in the brain and body, I believe these imbalances result from prolonged use of disequilibrium states.

A client came for help for his debilitating bouts of colitis. It was found that he had a lifestyle of either "hard charging" or "laziness", as he put it. These were the only two options he could consider. But each choice carried harmful consequences. Counseling helped him utilize a more moderate state in his life. Various early life circumstances led him to believe that just being effective in any task was not good enough. He set up a frame of "chase the infinite" and "achieve perfection".

The chase for perfection is never complete, since perfection can never be reached.

But the chase was exhausting and caused him a lot of physical pain through self-pressure and judgment. He literally got his bowels into an uproar. He suffered from the effects of irritable-bowel syndrome. Counseling helped him remove the discomfort by utilizing a moderate state. In his case, "competence". He could then hold a positive self-concept and utilize this state from within rather than try to generate a state through his achievements.

As another example of the bipolar effect, consider people who have led lives of substance abuse and impulsive self-destructive behavior. "Suddenly", they find religion. I do not mean spirituality, but the *dogma* of religion. They then adopt this lifestyle with equal zeal rather than the trademark peaceful humility of spirituality. It is not integrated within the person. They still do not see the midrange as available. They simply live this "new" script with the same fervor they had applied to substance abuse and other forms of self-abuse.

The untouchables: thoughts

This leads to just a few thoughts about the concept of chemical imbalances that supposedly bring on or cause mental disorders. In this tangible world, generally, if you can measure a substance it is the by-product of a process. You may be able to observe the process but you cannot measure it directly. Only its output or its change from A to B is measurable.

This limitation in our ability to measure plays out in the process that forms clouds and the precipitation that falls from them. We can measure the amount of rain but we can only label the cloud or source. We give clouds such labels as "nimbus", "cumulus", and "cumulonimbus". The process can be labeled ("condensation" and "precipitation") but it still cannot be measured because it is active and not static.

Measurements convey only the static part of a process. The specific ingredients that combine to create any given process can be removed from context, identified, and measured. But the interaction process, the dynamics, cannot be measured, only observed or experienced. Similarly, we cannot measure the process that occurs in a state of mind. Only the characteristics can be described and labeled. The process producing measurable chemical by-products is simply the result of utilizing various states of being. All science can do is wait for the outcome and measure it, sealed off from the intangible experience of the state.

Some groundbreaking research by David McClelland (1988) reveals the effects of mental states on the body's biochemistry. In one study, internally generating and experiencing altruistic thoughts significantly increased the presence of the antibody IgA, which fights off upper respiratory illness. In another instance, Herbert Benson MD has worked with the "relaxation response" in his research (Benson, 1976). The relaxation response is the body's response to deep states of relaxation. It has been documented that measurable increases occur in the amount of endorphins and other feel-good chemicals in people when they experience a deep state of relaxation.

Whether the chemical in question is serotonin or some other influential antibody or brain chemical, the level of this seems to come from the mental state of the person. We can alter the mental state by ingesting medications designed to control the level of certain chemicals in the body, but we can also alter the levels of the chemicals by changing the state of the person. In general, isn't something tangible the result of something intangible? The restricting scientific dogma that says it matters only if you can measure it leads us to a faulty conclusion, owing to faulty beliefs and limited measuring abilities. This in principle is the process that yields our limiting beliefs about self, believing the information that comes through our limited perception is all the information out there.

We are at the mercy of our measurement abilities, yet mistakenly believe these abilities capture all information.

Think of the universe as being like a movie. Science has only a camera with which to take photographs of this ongoing movie. We can compare two or more photos to measure the change, but we cannot measure the process because the process is ongoing and science can take only excerpts.

Within the human body there seems two roads on which to create change. Just as there are two "royal roads" to altering human states, kinesthetic and linguistic (Hall, 1995, 2000), it seems two roads exist for altering body chemistry: changing mental states and altering the kinesthetic status. Changing physical sensations (kinesthetic), for example, permits the beneficial results from relaxation training.

By deeply and systematically relaxing our muscles we can and do change mental states as long as we consider that new state a safe one. When we experience the meta-stating process, corresponding kinesthetic changes follow. The sensations alter as we go reach higher and higher Meta-States^R, from something like heavy or cold sensations to warm, light, and tingling sensations associated with reaching more resourceful Meta-States^R.

A state of mind can and does create measurable changes in body chemistry.

I have used this process of change in physical sensation in working with clients who experience chronic pain, when one of the skills I teach is to achieve a deeply relaxed state. Clients report significant pain relief from this simple process and often report a total *absence* of pain. A state of mind can and does create measurable changes in body chemistry. The process that generates this chemical change is not measurable. You can measure before and after relaxing but you can experience only the change process.

Chaos theory

We now return to the process of how people respond when they believe a state of equilibrium is unavailable, which leads to developing a bipolar-like appearance. People who seek and create chaos in their lives are a good example of this general response style. We find that these people actually seek calmness or a similar state. However, they come to believe that they can achieve calmness through chaos. Of course this doesn't work, but previous history drives the mistaken belief.

Very often people who seem to "need" chaos come from a family of origin in which chaos was a common event. Maybe the home life went beyond chaos. Perhaps one parent was an alcoholic. Whenever some lull in the action did occur the child might experience calm. This calm would be short-lived, and soon broken by either an alcohol-induced outburst or fallout from past behavior in the alcohol-abusing syndrome. All hell seems to break loose just when he starts to feel good, and soon he learns to avoid experiencing calm.

The child may have at one time naturally experienced an internal state of calm, but he soon finds that it does not feel safe to feel calm.

The state known as calm then becomes associated with feeling unsafe. Oddly, now chaos appears as the most feasible avenue for experiencing calm. Holding life in a constant state of flux feels safer. It helps him avoid the now dangerous state of calm. He comes to believe that if things settle down, even in his adult life, that somehow a huge conflict will happen, so he might choose a state of being "unsettled" as the next best option.

This state of being unsettled produces behavioral choices that lead to consistent chaos. In a weird way this may actually allow a greater sense of the state known as control, since the person chooses or dictates his environment, chaotic though it may be. He believes that experiencing calm creates a dangerous environment-chaos. The result is a structure of states something like a state of unsettledness, which supposedly leads to control, which is designed to bring calm. The intent of the logic is that through utilizing the state of unsettledness the person will feel more control and this will lead to a sense of calm. The actual result is that by utilizing the state of unsettledness he will experience chaos, less control, and little calm in his life or himself.

The level at which the problem exists for this person is at the state of calm. His hope is that by concocting a sophisticated strategy for protecting calm he will experience calm. However, this tactic also prevents him from utilizing calm himself. Because he hides the state of calm, others cannot disrupt this state, as his dad did. But the unsettled one doesn't have access to the state of calm, either. As a metaphor, the owner of a safety deposit box locks the key to the box in the box so no one else can get the goods. We lock ourselves out of our own goods.

Experiencing calm through anything other than calm does not yield calm. This principle holds for any and all states. Sometimes people try to access and utilize a state indirectly, for example, gaining calm through unsettledness. But this never pays off. Meta-stating the state of calm for this person would result in strengthening and securing calm by tying it to other higher and more powerful states. The state of calm felt vulnerable because he was still looking at the state with the perceptual errors he had in childhood. By raising the state of calm to higher levels of consciousness, meta-stating, he can now gain a higher developmental perspective, leaving behind the old perceptual constrictions associated with calm. He can utilize this higher state with his adult perception.

The states above the level of the problem solve the problem. Sometimes people place a buffer state between the endangered state and the environment, but this only complicates and perpetuates the problem. Why do we innately seem to occupy first the more primitive or primary states below the state at which the distress occurs?

Apparently, in order to perceive a threat to any state we must believe that the environment holds the power over the state's wellbeing. This point of view accompanies lower developmental levels, conformist and below. Thus we seek protection from the source, the environment. In response to this belief we place protective states between our felt endangered state and the external environment. If that first line of defense does not provide what we seek we will apply another layer between the first defense and the environment. We can liken this apparently innate process of protecting states to the fight-or-flight response (Cannon, 1932). We simply apply the process to states to preserve them.

We can liken this apparently innate process of protecting states to the fight-or-flight response.

Walter Cannon identified the fight-or-flight response in the 1920s during his research with animals' responses to stress. It is an ancient process and serves as a survival mechanism. When we perceive a threat to us in our environment the adrenal gland provides us with a burst of adrenaline. We use this fight-or-flight mechanism in operating our states when responding to a perceived threat. We may decide to fight (pull self and environment together), turning up the state for overpowering the enemy— assertive shifts to aggressive. The other option is flight, pushing self away from the environment and the threat we perceive within it. We use the adrenaline rush to run away to safety. This means we retreat or turn down the state to a less pronounced degree. Here, assertiveness takes flight and passivity steps in between the individual and her environment. In essence, we apply this phenomenon to states and find state survival mechanisms. We inflate the state or it runs and hides. Now we see the basis of aggressive or passive expression common to all states of disequilibrium. We either turn a state up and fight or turn it lower and flee.

This process of protecting various states relates to Loevinger's (1976) developmental stage of self-protection. This strategy takes place when a person puts a disengaging or blocking state between the environment and the believed endangered state within her. She protects self and the state within. The shy person places shyness between unrestricted self-expression and the environment. This way she permits some engaging, but it is with another internal state, shyness, and not the environment. The environment feels too unsafe.

As a result of efforts to protect self, people use various primary states of disequilibrium rather than the more capable and advanced state of equilibrium in order to interact with the world. The better-suited equilibrium states become muffled and contorted. The self-protective person essentially consists of a broad display of unbalanced primary states designed to protect his supposedly vulnerable states within.

Revisiting developmental stages

Humans progress through developmental stages in a similar manner to how an ameba moves itself, a bit at a time. We each contain some aspects of self that are quite well developed. The same person also carries within him some pockets of what seem rather retarded behavior, lagging behind in development compared with the rest of the person. The developmental lags we display are a form of self-protection. They are not coincidental or unexplainable lags *per se*. Rather, they point to unresolved internal wounds and the innate self-protecting process. The possible exception to this is the person who leads such a sheltered life that an absence of stimulation deprives him of opportunities to develop.

Once an emotional injury happens, an unconscious process brings a decision to preserve the equilibrium state by utilizing a defensive disequilibrium state.

This disequilibrium state acts as a buffer between the individual and the environment. The buffer is some form of exaggerated equilibrium state in a turned-up or turned-down form. While this person could turn to the state of passivity for the buffer, more often the self-protecting person utilizes states in the amplified form, such as aggression. Such people tend to display the "taker" style of operating. This stems the fear tide at the same time.

Because this "taker" strategy reduces fear, it becomes reinforced. As a result of this "success" at reducing fear, the person now employs this strategy of aggressive behavior for future challenges. Sometimes after experiencing success for a while by using aggression, she will meet with a situation where her level of aggressiveness does not work. She will then just escalate her aggressiveness, since it used to work up to this point. If some is good, remember, more is better.

Beyond the self-protective level is the conformist. Conformists generate more creative ways for managing unresolved issues. They find more socially approved states and place them in front of equilibrium states. Such people deny themselves awareness of their unique self in order to conform. Conformists most often utilize the opposite strategy of the self-protective person. They seem prone to filing down individuality so as to blend in smoothly and receive the sought approval. Their primary-state buffer exists in the more turned-down version such as passivity or agreeableness. The person who conforms to social expectations is most conforming in the areas where unresolved issues still reside. For example, she may find it easy to utilize assertiveness with strangers or even friends. But when it comes to utilizing assertiveness with her parents she still retreats into passivity.

She may also possess pockets of even less developed areas of self, showing these to only a few select people. This very retarded pocket may bring with it some form of self-destructive behavior, substance abuse or shoplifting, for example. She may lead a double life due to these unresolved issues. In general, these especially lagging parts of self may take the form of rebellious behavior. But do not confuse rebellion with constructive social action. The former plays a detrimental role to self and/or others, the latter benefits and betters *both* self and others.

Some other facets of this same person may show significant advancement well beyond the rebellious or conforming styles. The advanced parts evidence a healthy resource state for yet-to-be-resolved issues. We find the solution to how to evolve the developmentally delayed parts of self by determining how the more developed parts reached such higher development. Which beliefs, perceptions, values, purposes, or states permitted higher development? You can then borrow or apply these to evolve to "lagging" areas.

We all possess within us the capacity for significant development.

We manifest this regularly and collectively. We need only look to our own best parts or efforts for evidence. Uncovering and re-covering rather than installing parts is the task. Promoting human development is not necessarily a long and arduous process. We already contain all the essential ingredients.

We move now to the personality theory by Abraham Maslow, humanism (1962). Maslow took an unusual approach to studying human personality. Rather than study pathology, as psychological theories did before, Maslow chose to understand highly effective people and their personality. He wanted to find out how healthy people function so this could be duplicated.

Maslow held the belief that as humans we feel compelled to reach higher and higher forms of development. What we can become we must become, he said. This principle displays itself when we resourcefully find ways of expressing our states of equilibrium such as persistence, hope, calm, or peace. You cannot not persist at something! Even the laziest person in the world (although I'm not sure what kind of contest determines this!) uses incredible persistence, applied to laziness.

What we can become we must become. You cannot *not* persist at something!

All the states of equilibrium function as resource states for directly acting on some situation in the environment or within ourselves as a meta-state. We may love our hate, hate our fear (the basis of "hate crimes", which might be more accurately named "fear crimes"), feel satisfied with dissatisfaction, engage the state of withdrawal, or feel hopeful about the state of depression.

We must, as we have discussed, utilize a positive state to activate a negative state. Therefore, our drive to utilize our equilibrium still gets satisfied, just indirectly. When we believe that something in our environment endangers our state of equilibrium, we cover the state in a veil of disequilibrium, a limiting state. But we will still express our states of equilibrium rather than leave them dormant. Expressing them seems to be an undeniable human drive. Does this imply we are inherently good? Let your highest Meta-States[R] of equilibrium decide.

Regardless of what state we use for dealing with the environment, we still draw on and utilize equilibrium states. These principles apparently apply to any and all states. We may notice this process playing out in states such as pessimism. The pessimist feels optimistic that pessimism will keep him safe from disappointment. How's that for logic? Other states, such as indecisiveness, impulsiveness, arrogance, or any of the primary states, can serve as buffers between equilibrium and the environment.

Looking at the world through the lens of a limiting state carries with it the foibles of childhood perception. Limiting or negative states taint our perception of the environment by leading us to experience the world through egocentrism, transductive reasoning, inductive logic, centration, overgeneralizing, irreversibility, and thinking in absolutes (either all good or all bad). When our coping styles are based on this perception, we accidentally invite perceiving styles that complicate our life. This actually preserves the problem state rather than freeing the equilibrium for applying directly on the environment.

The drive to use the midrange states is incessant, so we feel compelled to express such states.

We sometimes come to believe we cannot directly fulfill our need. When state utilization is blocked, the issue is not so much that we seek to use buffers between an equilibrium state and the environment, but the specific developmental level at which we decide the need exists.

The level of development at which we recruit a negative state to act as a buffer determines how this process plays out. When did the SEE happen? The level of development at which the SEE occurs plays a crucial role in the type and use of the buffer state. Buffers manifest differently at various levels of development. The earlier the SEE, the more primitive the primary state chosen as the buffer, and the more it will possess extreme and rigid versions of the Piaget thought categories. These defenses are all we have at the time to protect the self. We always make the best use and best choice with what we are aware of at any given time.

As an analogy, in less "developed" areas of the world people use relatively primitive materials and methods to make buildings. These structures often lack stability and durability. It is not that these people know about more sophisticated methods but don't use them. Rather, they simply do not yet know about these methods. We can use only those methods that we know of and if we have access to the resources to use them. What methods do we of the supposed "developed" nations not yet know?

The point is that the level of human development at which the SEE occurs greatly determines the type and sophistication of the defensive state.

As additional cognitive-intellectual development happens, more sophisticated buffers come into place. For example, this produces a more cunning criminal or a more complex "neurosis". If the original wound is not healed, and SEEs repeat over time, then the more sophisticated cognitive skills that come with human development will simply take the form of Meta-States^R bent on protecting and preserving the originally "injured" state in its primitive form. The making of a "personality disorder" begins here. This is more accurately referred to as personality disordering, a process of *disordering* the original structure of the personality.

If significant development happens before any SEE, buffers are not as necessary, if necessary at all. It seems that unconsciously chosen primary-state buffers reveal their developmental functioning level through their primary-state style. The primary state of disequilibrium used for protecting the equilibrium state correlates to a developmental level.

For example, a young child may use rage to protect a state of happiness if he feels his happiness threatened. An older child may use a protective state in line with his need to gain approval from others. He may respond with socially acceptable assertiveness when he feels a threat to his happiness. Therefore, the primary defense state also reveals the general time of the emotional injury. While this is not a new idea, I believe this age-defense-state correlation remains true.

Usually, the more extreme the maladaptive coping state is, the earlier was the SEE.

We usually develop misconceptions about our world during our early childhood, roughly the first seven years. After all, our earliest maps of the world are made through perceptual lenses that operate from very limited cognitive abilities. The misperceiving leads to misconceptions or very poor maps of the world. We attribute our states to the environment and others in it and then strike back against any believed offender. These acts vary only in degrees and range from self-deprivation through verbal abuse of others to nuclear war.

This misattribution of power seems to be an essentially innate perceptual style accompanying the first few levels of human development. Some change can come after early childhood, age eight to eleven, but even this is limited more than in the later years. With adolescents or adults, one way to bring about a change in relations between the individual and the environment is to access beliefs about the relationship between self and the all-powerful environment, then identify the state behind these beliefs and meta-state the state. This brings a perceptual shift, returning state control and choice back within the individual.

Let's use an example of restructuring relations with the environment and states within. I worked with a client who wanted to lose a significant amount of weight. She found that three particular states drove her overeating: boredom, anger, and depression. Of particular relevance here is the work we did with her state of depression. During the meta-stating process she found that the absence of depression led to a state she called comfort. The state of comfort, when fully experienced, led to a state she called emotional independence. Here we see she just turned the tables on "cause–effect".

She is no longer affected internally by external events. I asked what happened to anger at this state of emotional independence and she said it was also gone. We then went to the state that she found when she experienced total emotional independence: control. This process continued until she reached a state that she called happy. From this state we reviewed the situations in which she'd previously felt depressed or angry and had responded by eating. She now felt very different and this different state carried with it very different perceptions. She could now see that her emotions were separate from the events. This awareness enabled her to choose her states and in the process feel more able to choose what and when to eat.

No state is ever given or taken by the environment. We just believe our states are fragile and abandon them under perceived danger.

It always remains our choice to stay or go, but so often the choice takes place unconsciously, from a limited perceptual vantage and, therefore, we incorrectly attribute cause and effect.

Chapter Eight
The Structure of Personality: It's Just a State of Mind

With the ingredients of our personality and their dynamics identified, we will now examine the general structure of human personality. I will not attempt to describe each and every feature of our personality or go through every diagnosis. I will give a general description of what I believe to be the driving forces and consequences at work in our personality.

As we saw earlier, our personality originates with access to all states. By nature we begin operating from states of equilibrium. We naturally gravitate toward a balance within our personality while allowing ourselves to roam the continuum. This gives us free movement to any and all primary and Meta-States^R.

I like the concept of abandon to describe our original nature. One meaning of the word "abandon" is "unrestrained freedom of action or emotion". To me this concept represents the very nature of us a species. This unrestrained freedom of action or emotion is how we start in life and what we seek to regain if we experience distress. In this case, the unrestrained freedom relates to accessing our states.

We can think of the structure of states as being like a tall building. Though, with meta-states the sky is the limit, not the top story of the building. No metaphor is exact or complete, but this one will do as a general representation. Imagine a building so tall that its top is out of sight. Within this building exist various stories and a glass elevator at the front. In this elevator you can ride up and down to the different floors while still looking out over the whole environment. Notice the view of the outside increasing with height.

Once you reach your desired floor, you may go to any office or suite you care to visit. There reside information and resources fitting a myriad circumstances, representing the various Meta-States^R. You access what you need and then return to the ground floor and go out of the building into the environment. Once out of the building you implement your plan of action, utilizing the states and resources you got from within. This strategy's design is to bring about the desired outcome in the environment.

Personal impairment plays out in this analogy by having a limited elevator with certain floors blocked off and perhaps various offices and suites off-limits to us. You have probably heard it said of a person who seems a bit mentally lacking that his or her elevator doesn't go to the top floor. Well, the meaning here is a little different. The elevator may not go to the top floor or may not stop at certain floors, which represents self-limiting beliefs. Some of us may even have a phobia about elevators. The result limits us to certain states, many of which may only be primary states.

Our response to the belief that a state is blocked is governed by the perceptual limitations that led us to believe the state is dangerous. The same Piagetian thought styles that led us to believe mistakenly that a state is dangerous now try to show us the solution choices! How can this possibly lead us to an effective solution? When we believe a state of equilibrium is blocked we tend to respond in an either/or thinking style. From this point on, the box of options only shrinks.

As we have seen, we either amplify the state we believe we cannot occupy or turn down the volume. The original state modifies into another state once it's turned up or down. Assertiveness becomes aggression or passivity respectively. If some is good more is better. As a result, we become more aggressive or passive if and when the original compensating strategy feels threatening to us.

The best way to solve the problem is by "going meta" to it, thereby accessing additional resources and altered perception. People will change always and only for a higher meta level. But those with personality disorders apparently cannot permit themselves to access their full complement of resources lest they endanger their entire being. They are taught this at an early age. Internal resources, other than to feed the disorder, are not permitted for these people.

We've previously discussed the concepts of "asker" and "taker". The "asker" lowers self-respect and asks others to meet his needs. He spends a lot of time hoping his needs will be met rather than assertively pursuing them himself. The "taker" pressures people to give him what he needs. He disrespects others and preys on or imposes on them to some degree. Mild forms of asking-taking make up classic neuroses while its extremes make up the personality disorders. You can think of the "asker-taker" as existing on a continuum like the pursuer/distancer in relationships or to the introvert/extrovert concept (Jung, 1953).

The "asker" is similar to the "flight" element of Cannon's fight-or-flight concept while the "taker" is like the "fight" element.

The "asker" is similar to the "flight" part of Cannon's fight-or-flight process in that he withdraws from and does not directly pursue his goal. The "taker" is like the "fight" element as he actively pursues his goal. A third category in the fight-or-flight concept was added later: "freeze". "Freezing" is also a form of asking in that the one who freezes does not actively pursue his needs. This particular set of responses, ask/take, steers the direction in which the person moves in response to perceiving a state of equilibrium as unavailable.

The taker chooses more outgoing responses and actively pursues her needs. She likely displays less tolerance for and frustration of her needs. Her overall strategy involves more assertive and possibly aggressive means of taking what she needs from others. The taker's challenge may be that of how to respect others. For the "taker" to satisfy her needs she must find an "asker".

These two strategies serve as the foundation for response styles when we cannot operate from equilibrium states. The various degrees of asking/taking are arranged with corresponding diagnoses in the table below. Keep in mind that there exists a mild, moderate, and severe version of each personality-disordering diagnosis. But in this table, I give a general ranking for the disorders in terms of the asker-taker continuum. Also notice that the diagnosis of passive-aggressive qualifies for each side of the continuum. This is because the person using this style fluctuates between the asker and taker poles of the continuum.

Table 8.1: The asking-taking continuum and corresponding diagnoses

Extreme asking	Extreme taking
——————————————— Equilibrium ———————————————	
Diagnoses	Diagnoses
Borderline Dependent	Histrionic Narcissistic
Schizoid	Antisocial
Paranoid	Paranoid
Obsessive-compulsive	Obsessive-compulsive
Passive-aggressive	Passive-aggressive

The table displays the asker-taker strategies and the resulting personality disordering below the line. The further toward the endpoints of the continuum, the more extreme are the thoughts, emotions, and behavior. Also keep in mind that none of the personality disorders seen here act independently. They cluster together, though usually one feature of the cluster predominates the person's style. The individual diagnoses within the class of conditions known as personality disorders never travel alone. A person displaying a dependent style will almost certainly utilize passive-aggressive tendencies as well as histrionic, avoidant, and possibly some borderline ones, along with obsessive-compulsive ways. The narcissistic style also utilizes paranoia, antisocial behavior, histrionic, ways and often obsessive-compulsive and passive-aggressive processes.

A person displaying a dependent personality style will almost certainly utilize passive-aggressive tendencies as well as avoidant and possibly some borderline tendencies.

Likewise, the obsessive-compulsive and passive-aggressive personality can occupy both the "asker" and the "taker" position. She feels such a strong need to do so much for so many people in such a perfect way. She often asks for her needs to be met by doing for others. But, after a time spent in the unrealistic world of believed achievable perfection, frustration sets in and she snaps, becoming a "taker". She then shifts to the passive-aggressive personality style.

How can we be so sure these disordering by-products travel in clusters? The basis for choosing to utilize these disordered states comes from a survival mechanism for the organism. An extreme trauma or series of traumas jolts the person to these extremes of function. In response to a trauma that feels like a life-threatening situation, the person takes no chances. If he believes he will die if he directly expresses himself, the many efforts in multiple forms must take place to ensure survival. Once she has left equilibrium to such an extreme, the person enters the pool of personality-disorder styles. Though the surface behavior may differ within personality-disorder styles, they have a common root: abandonment of the individuated unique self. As a protective device to keep the self alive, self is abandoned and other thought and behavioral styles come to the "rescue".

The borderline personality must not only hide his true internal self for its protection but must then recruit paranoia as a guard for potential threats. Additional needs include good organizational skills to prevent straying from this narrow path, permitting some semblance of safety. This is where the obsessive-compulsive *disorder* (OCD)—not the obsessive-compulsive *personality*—commonly teams up with personality disorders. Combining the process of borderline personality with OCD provides some semblance of structure to the felt, essential, tightly knit, narrow range of behaviors. The OCD makes for some predictable rituals that both lend structure to an otherwise chaotic life and provide an outlet for some of the very high anxiety.

Borderline personalities perceive the territory to either side of their narrow path as fraught with landmines. The presence of panic attacks is also quite common in borderline personalities. How else could it be, given their beliefs about the lethal danger of many states? Perceiving so many triggers or tripwires gives reason for panic attacks. The borderline personality and the narcissistic personality are the two extremes of asking and taking, respectively. You might think of each of these two disorders as being the inverse of the other. The borderline and narcissist both have urgent needs. But they generally go about meeting them in different ways. The borderline begs and feels unworthy, taking out frustration on herself. The narcissist believes she is entitled to having her needs met by others and more likely takes out her frustration on others. But either disorder may manifest alternating or singular versions of the two response poles (asker-taker).

The other personality disorders, such as passive-aggressive, dependent, or obsessive-compulsive, are merely less extreme versions of borderline or narcissistic disordering. The common thread running through all is fear of associating into certain states, ultimately the self, along with grief over perceiving the loss of certain states.

Each personality strategy used represents the best attempt a person can make, given he believes he is not free to access the self. For example, passive-aggressive is a bipolar on the freedom-seeking continuum. They may constantly choose from an array of options but never commit to just one. They do this in an attempt to verify their freedom. Believing his freedom fragile, a person makes an all-consuming efforts to verify it. He experiences at once anxiety over associating into freedom and depression over feared loss of freedom.

The result of this tug-of-war makes him a prisoner of his search for freedom. He ends up using the freedom-preserving process on himself by never committing, rather than using his freedom to structure his environment more successfully in order to reach his goals. A classic self-imposed double bind rules him. As a result, freedom eludes the self while being consumed with verifying its existence. Essentially, freedom can never be utilized to reach a goal other than to prove its existence—a dizzying loop.

The following is a brief allegory to illustrate the principles of freedom for freedom's sake.

He experiences at once, anxiety over associating into the state of freedom and depression over the feared loss of freedom. He becomes imprisoned by his search for freedom that he can never allow himself to possess.

Prisoner of the sea

Once there was a man, or maybe it was a woman. It could have been either because what this person did was more important than who he or she was. This person was determined to be free and experience this feeling. Living in a coastal town, he grew up watching the sea. What great appeal the sea had for him, never still, always in motion, seemingly boundless. Many people sailed into the town's port but would set out to sea not long after arriving. This seemed the good life, never stuck in one place, seeing a lot of different places and people. *Wow!* This is freedom. The remainder of his childhood was spent longing to live the life of a sailor of the seas, riding the open waves.

Finally of age, he joined up with a ship's crew and set out to sea. He thrived on the experience and became quite an expert at sailing the oceans, docking at ports, and returning to sea. He excelled at his work and eventually owned a ship of his own. Now he was really free and in control! He came and went as he pleased, whenever and wherever he found a way to justify a trip by carrying cargo.

Day after day, week after week, year after year, he never stopped in one port for too long. There was always another place for him to go to, all the while experiencing his freedom. Gradually, it became apparent that he could not stay in any one port even if he wanted to. Freedom now dictates the moves. If too much settling occurred he felt obliged to leave. Otherwise he would lose his freedom—or so his thinking went.

He actually met and grew fond of many people and longed to see them again. Duty always called, though, requiring him to return to the sea. Now he felt compelled to leave what had begun to be fulfilling—connecting more deeply to others. But maintaining his freedom remained a necessity. Staying in port and off the sea meant losing control and freedom. He became a prisoner of the sea.

As with all coins, this freedom coin has another side. The other side of the freedom coin reveals a strategy of preserving freedom by refusing to choose. This refusal to choose operates on the belief that, if you do not declare a choice, others cannot take your choice from you or use your exposed need against you. So you save up all your choices, keeping them in a safe. The problem with this strategy is that you can't spend any of the money while locked in the safe with it. Choosing not to choose in order to preserve your freedom only deprives you of using your freedom more flexibly.

Now we come back to land after our story. We have been describing some of the general processes present in the category of diagnoses called personality disorders. These diagnoses actually refer to the by-product of depriving oneself of access to states of equilibrium. Personality-disordered people believe they cannot operate from the midpoints of traits such as assertiveness, self-expression, or a host of moderate states, because the midpoints equate to a display self. Early lessons taught these people that the use of self is forbidden. If they dare go there and utilize the resources within self, then the all-powerful parents will extinguish them.

The personality disordering comes from believing that the infinite resources of the self are off-limits. Personality-disordered people cannot form beliefs about self of a first-hand nature. They only get to hear about how terrible it would be to access self. Thinking about occupying self, let alone actually operating self, is blasphemy. From this point, compensating behaviors take over.

Perceiving permanent lockout from self, the child institutes a series of efforts designed to make the best of a bad situation. The mind needs soothing as much as anything. It struggles with the awareness of what feels like necessary personal limitations. The mental and emotional pain of this distress stimulates various responses.

The one commonality that personality-disordered persons seem to have is that they tend to seek comfort from external sources rather than from within.

These ailing personality-disordered people tend to reside in one primary state after another and only occasionally use Meta-States^R. Doing so functions only as a slightly more elaborate strategy for gaining a modicum of relief from external sources rather than from self. The personality structure is a massive defense mechanism that prevents others from accessing and manipulating but it also blocks access to the owner of self.

The personality-disordered person organizes all states in order to not access the self.

Compensation for not accessing self consists of an elaborately disguised use of self through others—vicarious living at its worst. The disordered person orchestrates his choices in a manner designed to meet his needs and ease his fears of feeling disconnected from the resourceful self. He accomplishes this by persuading others into meeting his needs. The "asker" or "taker" position comes into play here in fairly extreme forms. This is how those with personality disorders seem so resourceful or appear to be such effective survivors. They react with great survival skills, but can initiate nothing that gives away or reveals use of self. They actually operate the self exceptionally well but do not know this because it is accomplished indirectly. Other people are asked to meet, or manipulated into meeting, the disordered one's needs.

The inevitable expression of equilibrium

As we saw earlier, we cannot keep from using our equilibrium states. The difference is whether we utilize them directly or cloak them in disequilibrium states. It seems that all dis-equilibrium states necessarily draw their activation from equilibrium states. Consider the person who desires to engage others yet fears that state of engaging others because of associated memories. Cleverly, he still finds a way to engage others. He just hides behind the state known as shyness, inhibition, or something similar. In order to *display* the state of shyness, one first needs to *engage* the state of shyness. Inevitably it seems we must live from and apply our adaptive states, including our larger infinite self.

Believing a state to be endangered moves us to take up shields to preserve it. But when do we know it is safe to come out from behind the shield? And, more importantly, what misconception leads us to think anything could ever endanger our states? Our states are intangible and immune to any and all earthly forces. But when we believe our states to be fragile we then compensate for "wounds". In some sense, then, dysfunction is nothing more than compensating for the illusion that we can be wounded in the first place.

Personality-disordered individuals are masters of developing and using compensatory methods. They frequently engage in substance abuse to numb the awareness of their compromising position and associated anxiety and depression. Awareness of even indirect access to self activates intense anxiety at best. The dilemma then is how to balance the delicate interaction with the environment, others as a resource, the resulting internal disequilibrium, and the conscious and unconscious belief that utilizing self will be deadly. From the personality-disordered person's perspective, all of life provides potential opportunities to utilize self, so all of life also provides the potential for stepping on a landmine. Potential danger lurks at every turn. No wonder almost all personality disordering brings intense anxiety.

Depression also naturally accompanies the personality-disordering process. It may manifest overtly or covertly. It may show itself on the surface, being readily apparent. But this is only the tip of the "depression-berg". It achieves sufficient size to rip gaping holes in any seemingly seaworthy state of equilibrium launched from the self. This permits only the smallest of dinghies the opportunity for sailing. In other words, the depression allows only so much self-initiative and success. Beyond a certain threshold of accomplishment or individuation, the individual would sever the cord that connects the lifeline to the powers that be, probably her parents in this case. She already believes that disconnecting from the parentally imposed, limiting beliefs leads to certain demise of self. How can she then not feel vulnerable and anxious? It seems the only way to combat this is to limit achievement in any form.

The dynamics of anxiety and depression

We will now differentiate between the states of depression and anxiety. They do not necessarily develop only within the personality-disordering process. These two states exist as Meta-States^R, forming the foundation for any type of dysfunction. Depression and anxiety are by-products of our relationship with our various states. That is, they are states representing thoughts or feelings about other states. In fact we find their dynamics exist in some sense as opposites of each other.

Depression and anxiety are by-products of our relationship with our various states.

Anxiety occurs because the person doesn't want to associate into a particular state. He believes that the feared state carries with it some potential for emotional pain such as disapproval and rejection from others. This anxiety-provoking state remains associated with some past aversive outcome. As a result, the individual attempts to move around and avoid this state at all costs.

The anxiety I describe here is not like the fear we experience at the zoo when we notice the lion's cage door is open and there is no lion in sight. This event at the zoo is real life-threatening danger. Oddly, anxiety operates like visiting the zoo but noticing the door to the lion's cage (feared state) is closed with the lion in the cage. But anxiety takes what is factually true and then speculates from there. Anxiety revolves around what *could* happen (the lion might escape) rather than what is happening (the lion is in his cage). The fear stems from either a particular significant emotional event in the past that could happen again but is not happening now, or what that past event almost became. The word "almost" in this situation makes the person act as if the event *had* happened, whereas, in the literal sense, "almost happened" is similar to "did not happen" in that, either way, there was no event.

When producing anxiety we essentially become phobic about the particular state. Drawing on the Piaget category of overgeneralizing, we then scan each situation we encounter looking for similarities to the adverse event. When a person notices an item in the environment similar to the actual frightening event, thus providing potential to associate into the original event, anxiety begins. The frightened person uses far too broad a category to sort items so that all items colored blue, for example, come to remind him of the earlier traumatic event. This process of overgeneralizing is post-traumatic stress disorder (PTSD) in its essence. In some sense, the dynamics of PTSD form the foundation for any dysfunction. The person tries so hard to keep history from repeating, that he ends up with an anxiety-based disorder.

Anxiety amounts to a phobic reaction to a particular state.

Well-intended efforts, designed to help the person feel safe, actually lead the person to use what might be called ironic logic. These anxiety-preventing efforts lead us to lock ourselves in the lion's cage with the lion in it! The illogical thought process runs like this: "If I can keep my eye on the anxiety-provoking stimulus at all times, then I can keep tabs on what I fear. This will keep me safe." Unfortunately, this strategy only leads to increasing the level and frequency of anxiety. It seems we only get more of whatever is our focus.

When we focus on our fear we only feel more, even though this chosen focus is designed to decrease fear. Instead of looking for ways to experience safety, a person ends up finding reasons to experience fear. These reasons only meta-state the fear and make it worse. If this strategy continues, the person reaches a state of paralysis, as nearly everything becomes anxiety-provoking. This focus on fear is partly how we end up coming face to face with our deepest fears. The fear always stays on our mind, initiating choices that only lead to what we originally sought to prevent.

Case study
June fell while walking in a parking lot. She slipped on a small puddle of oil. She injured her back severely and required surgery. After this injury, she walked in great fear because she was always on the lookout for places where she might slip and fall. She believed danger was around every corner and that, if she even saw any potential danger, she was as good as already hitting the ground.

When she walked anywhere, inside or outside, she would scan the area for potential danger. This only provoked anxiety the whole time she walked. She could not let herself experience the equilibrium state of calm that she had been in before she fell. Her logic told her that, if she did experience calm, she would fall again. Safety took precedence. In order to experience any sense of calm, she would have to experience anxiety!

Even in the absence of any dangerous evidence, she could generate anxiety by thinking about what might happen. She came to perceive the very stimulus-provoking anxiety was surrounding her, at least potentially. To reach this point in the belief system, she had to ignore the middle links in a sequence of events. These middle links would have to happen for the dreaded event to happen. But she skipped over these middle steps and immediately associated step A with step Z. This process of going from point A straight to point Z is known as jumping to conclusions or inductive logic. And what do you jump over on the way to the conclusion? Facts that would lead to differentiating the fear from fact.

As the result of a SEE, the emotionally injured person develops a great need to detect features in the present that are similar to the past SEE circumstances.

He looks only for potential dangers. Once he finds any features common to the SEE, justifying the scan for danger, he then jumps to conclusions and anxiety happens. This process continues and can lead to panic and agoraphobia as convoluted coping skills designed to avoid dangerous situations. The feared state involves some state of equilibrium, perhaps calm.

A difference exists, though, between the personality-disorder type of anxiety—Type II, as we'll call it—and the nondisordered kind of anxiety—Type I. The previous case example represents a more situation-specific anxiety, not the type found in personality-disordered people. Type II anxiety is more pervasive, interfering with life on a larger scale. This deeper anxiety often revolves around expressing a personal skill or talent that would lead to significant accomplishments. This would amount to a display of the deeper unique self. In Type II, drawing from and utilizing one's unique self equates to certain rejection by significant others. The isolation that would follow the rejection amounts to a near-death experience. The idea of ceasing to exist generates extreme amounts of anxiety that are decreased only by backing down from self-expression.

Here, with Type I anxiety, the purpose is to find safe pathways to reach goals but instead only notices potentially dangerous items.

Type I anxiety is the state used to scan the environment for safety or danger about a relatively small collection of stimuli. The purpose of this anxiety-driven scan is to develop and use more successful behaviors that *do* permit expressing the true self—essentially the opposite of Type II anxiety. Type I, a less extreme sort of anxiety than Type II, manifests by reversing the focus of the original intent. Here, anxiety wants to determine safe pathways to reach goals but instead notices only dangerous or potentially dangerous obstacles. The intention of safe self-expression remains but the person blocks this self-expression accidentally by detecting only danger. In the personality disorder, the person blocks self-expression purposefully and as a self-preservation devise.

Depression

Now that we've defined and differentiated anxieties, let us look at the state of depression. just as two degrees of anxiety exist, two degrees of depression also exist. One type occurs after a bad out-come or an external loss—let us call it Type I depression. Type II depression, the personality disordered variety, results from a trained disconnection from and loss of true self. This type involves grief over abandoned states that are given up as a self-preservation mechanism.

In general, depression is a meta-state. It happens in response to an interaction with one or more of our states, representing how we feel about the safe use of a particular state. Differentiating more between anxiety and depression, we find they are essentially opposite responses to relations about states. Anxiety involves fear of utilizing an available taboo state. Trying to avoid an available but dangerous state is anxiety. Trying to utilize a state believed unavailable brings depression. But the commonality between anxiety and depression is that each stems from a belief that a person should not utilize the state in question. In the state of depression, a person mourns the loss of a state she felt compelled to abandon and a sense of loss then follows.

Depression results when a person wants to utilize an abandoned state but believes the state is lost forever.

Depression that results from the loss of a loved one, whether through death or a parting of the ways, reveals the deceased state being attributed to a person who died or moved on in some way. When the other person leaves, for whatever reason, it is believed that they take the state with them, leaving emptiness and loss of a state such as love or joy. Those people who rely on others for direction and let the environment dictate to them tend to find it harder to resolve depression in response to any form of loss.

Another way depression seems to come about is through a mis-guided internal search for a solution. In this case, the person com-mits some sort of mistake that leads to an undesired outcome. In response to this outcome, he abandons the state utilized at the time of the mistake. From this point he starts to look within himself for the solution rather than just adjusting his behavior. Rather than just taking a closer look at the way the issue was dealt with or the makeup of the issue, he puts egocentricity into action. With egocentricity he draws conclusions about himself and decides the state he was in at the time of the mistake is the mistake itself.

There was really no problem within him or the state, just a need to utilize environmental feedback and try a different approach. He threw the baby out with the bathwater. The dynamics of the event are misinterpreted so the search for a solution begins, but in the wrong place. Since no internal flaw really exists, no internal solution will be found. Judgment of self can start here if he believes he has a fault and can find a solution. He then finds fault with himself for not finding the fault!

Logical it isn't, but this is the depression-producing process that takes place once the self is condemned as being at fault. The sense of loss begins over abandoning a state and not finding a solution within self. This leads to an ever-deepening and downward-spiraling search within self and negative judgment of self. These steps then move the person further away from the solution and deeper into the vacuum that is depression.

The other scenario that breeds depression accompanies the dynamics of a personality-disordering process, Type II. This depression is a sort of internal-state "homicide" that takes place during childhood. The depressed person may have "killed" a state (happiness, for example) because some significant other told him that he must not utilize that state. If he utilizes happiness he will suffer the consequence of extreme rejection. Sometimes the person doing depression "kills" a state from a position of hope (remember, behind every state of depression is a state of hope) that the significant other will provide approval and, through this, permit a state of happiness to be experienced.

Any state of happiness the child seeks is granted by the significant other only as a result of the child's abandoning his own internal state of happiness. This granted happiness is conditional, based on submission to the significant other. Consider the person doing depression when he believes he is being rejected by a significant other. His fervent hope is that by depressing himself, somebody will come along and loan him the rejected state of "happiness" or at least move him away from "sadness". This accounts for his feeling "lost" when the significant other is not around. He might make statements such as, "I just can't feel happy when she is not around me." This sort of relationship arrangement forever limits the relationship. The depressed person can never generate his own happiness unless he wants to risk losing his significant other.

The deeper issue within a depressed person is the disconnecting that happens inside herself.

She disconnects from her true self and its infinite resources and states. When we connect to our true self we can access higher levels of development. Doing so takes us to meta-stating possibilities, leading to the ultimate meta-state that is limitless. Here the person looses depression because she gains free access to any and all states, feeling unified. This access is not limited to self, but at the ultimate state it transcends all levels of development, including the total universe. This relates to the seventh level of development noted by Lawrence Kohlberg (1969).

Kohlberg used moral reasoning as a means of measuring human development. He believed seven levels of development exist. At the highest level a person experiences a universal oneness. Few people reach and operate from this level. The religions of the world make reference to this state of unity with the universe. For example, Hindus refer to this feeling as *samadhi*. From the connecting that occurs at the highest level, the person also finds the required states and implements them in life.

Since depression is about self-imposed state limitations, it cannot exist when limits cease. Yes, this ultimate place includes depression on the menu as it includes any and every state. The difference here is that the person is free to choose the state he or she most deeply desires. What was the feeling you experienced the first time you no longer had to choose from the child's menu at a restaurant? Did you keep choosing from it or find you were now free to choose any item even though the child's menu was still in view?

Dysfunction involves either depression or anxiety as its central mechanism.

Depression and anxiety tend to form a sort of inverse relationship with each other. Given this essentially inverse relationship between depression and anxiety, we may conclude that dysfunction involves either depression or anxiety as its central mechanism. We are either *afraid* of associating into State X (anxiety), or *sad* we cannot associate into State X (depression). There are degrees of anxiety and depression depending upon the significance of the state and/or the number of states involved. The number of states abandoned usually relates to the number of steps the person takes in moving away from the original state of equilibrium.

Once the person has left the midrange of a state, any aversive events not effectively managed result in additional steps (turning up or down the state) away from the midrange. The highly anxious person has a high number of states that are off-limits and thus more and more situations provoke anxiety. Any situation in which the person could benefit from operating the taboo state (confidence for example) is sufficient for setting off anxiety, as he fears being sucked into associating. He tries his best to avoid situations that require using the feared state or states.

Does this mean "personality disorders" have their roots before age two? My initial suspicion is that these disorders occur due to a belief about self and the world from which the person cannot dissociate. This "flypaper-like" belief engages people and they apparently cannot shed its constriction. This seems to prevent access to most states of equilibrium. It is as if most states of equilibrium repel the individual. The limiting belief may be something like, "If I associate into my true self I will be completely rejected by my parent and surely die." The only way to survive the terror of certain death associated with being one's true self is to remain largely dissociated from the self.

Since the events that trigger his self-abandonment are perceived as life-threatening, the child never comes out of hiding to check on his safety.

The limiting belief clearly states that to save the self one must never operate from the self. However, the death of the self occurs because one does not operate from self. This simple coping or survival mechanism of dissociating from self may first happen when the child possesses this ability to dissociate as his only coping skill. Since the events that trigger his self-abandonment are perceived as life threatening, the child never comes out of hiding later in life to check on his safety. Any time he comes close to associating into his self, he re-experiences the original anxiety from the time of the trauma and feels in mortal danger all over again. He then permanently hides himself from his own resources. Thus, coping skills never evolve and he operates from an infantile level of thinking and coping.

This inverted logic appears in most unproductive coping mechanisms or diagnoses. A person fears that occupying the state of peace, for example, will cause peace to be lost or taken away by others. As a result she never goes there, only to experience anxiety or perhaps a state of panic. She longs for peace yet fears losing it, so she keeps herself from peace. She then fluctuates between a state of anxiety over nearly associatinginto peace and a state of depression over the believed loss of peace.

The choice made for preserving the state causes its unavailability. Oddly, she believes remaining in an anxious state will lead to peace but anything less than total peace will not *bring* total peace. She also believes that by not associating into peace she can protect the state of peace within her. But the sequence is wrong. Associating into peace actually protects the self. Resource states are not fragile. Dissociating from these resource states leaves the rest of the self feeling very fragile.

What leads to such a fear-filled belief that a person abandons the self? It may be that a significant trauma, whenever it occurs, is so severe the person actually believes dissociating from certain compensating states and associating into the self presents life-threatening danger. In either case, it is difficult to reach and teach the person to dissociate from these limiting beliefs. Deeply traumatized children seem to believe that accessing the richness of the self means certain self-destruction. As a result they block any and all points of entry into self. Extremely self-detrimental compensating mechanisms follow. Metaphorically, the person who fears drowning clings for dear life to what he believes is a floatation devise. But this turns out to be an anvil taking him to the very depths he wanted to avoid.

157

Severe depression results from moving multiple steps away from the original equilibrium states.

The person grieves her lost states and feels hope that depression will somehow bring her relief through others. Until she accesses and utilizes her own states, though, she will not stop depression. She will only find depression actually does bring others who "save" her. As a result, depressing self becomes reinforced, since it did justify the hope behind it.

The more severe the depression the more the number of states marked as lost. Severe anxiety and depression naturally accompany personality disordering, as such people greatly fear associating into self. They experience anxiety at the prospect of drawing on the resources of the self and so can't access this storehouse. The loss of self and the numerous resources within brings about severe depression over this loss. We can envision quite a tug of war going on inside the personality-disordered. They oscillate between anxiety and depression as they attempt the delicate balancing act. They fear accessing self, thus experience anxiety. Stemming the tide of anxiety means moving away from the self, but this strategy raises the levels of depression, owing to the loss of self.

A deeper look into states and emotional disorders

As a result of this anxiety–depression interplay in response to abandoned state, we now say that psychiatric diagnoses are simply statements about which and how many states the person fears he will enter (anxiety) or can't enter (depression). To illustrate the principles we will use the varying degrees of introversion and extroversion, with ambiversion as the equilibrium state.

A person fearing extroversion due to a SEE in his childhood might then act more inhibited in adulthood and get labeled as "quiet". If a more severe trauma occurs or repeats, he will move further left of equilibrium. He might then be considered shy. If this state encounters still more adversity then he may move further to the left and perhaps gain the label of "withdrawn". Each step moves the person further from the needed resources. If repeated aversive events, or one major event, occur in childhood, then the person may disengage from self to an even greater degree. This happens in the diagnosis of avoidant personality.

A state of retreat beyond the avoidant point of retreat is known as a schizoid personality disorder. Characteristics of this disorder include an essentially flat affect with a generally unresponsive style throughout life. These individuals come to fear self-expression greatly and therefore void themselves of almost all self-expression. Diagnoses simply exist as differing degrees of the same process; avoiding or losing a state and the compensating that follows becomes the symptom/diagnosis. What internal entity oversees this process of migrating from equilibrium? The self, naturally. However, the process takes place deep within the unconscious mind.

> **Diagnoses simply exist as differing degrees of the same process; avoiding or losing a state and the compensating that follows becomes known as the symptom/diagnosis.**

Another crucial element in emotional disorders deserves discussing here. Paranoia occurs in all anxiety- and depression-based disordering processes. Hall (1995, 2000) defines paranoia as fear of fear. I suggest the basis of anxiety is the need to avoid fearful states and the environmental circumstances that can possibly trigger these states. This is where paranoia enters the picture. People with any significant degree of anxiety must also fear their fear and essentially examine all situations for any possible fear-invoking circumstances. While paranoia appears to be a fear of something in the environment, it is really about fear of associating into a state triggered by the circumstance. This feared state has come to be linked with certain circumstances.

Paranoia is actually about fear of the fear that would happen by associating into a dangerous state. Encountering the fear of certain states becomes as frightening as the states themselves. Once again, we find higher-order conditioning (Pavlov, 1927) at work. In Piaget's terms, the paranoid person has *generalized* to an extreme. The result is fearing the fear that would spring from associating into certain states. Anxious people welcome paranoia as their security guard. It operates meta to the anxiety, forming a protective shield around any states that possess potential for invoking fear. But then the paranoid person imprisons himself with his paranoia.

The paranoid person does not just fear a particular state: he fears his fear of that state.

No doubt this mechanism serves as a distancing device, allowing greater feelings of safety. Now notice the dynamics of people who fear encounters with others in which self-expressing differences of opinion are called for. They fear even encountering the fear in the situation. They will not only avoid expressing a difference of opinion, but they will not place themselves in any situation where they think differences of opinion could happen. Avoidance is born. Their world takes a giant leap backward, shrinking as it goes.

Paranoia may also accompany depression. Paranoia works by fearing the fear of losing additional states in the process of depression. A protective mode akin to a shutdown or lockdown may occur if paranoia sets in. The purpose of this is to prevent further and future loss of states. The person closes and locks the door to his psyche, effectively shutting out others and shutting down operations within himself. This would require quite a serious SEE or multiple SEEs.

Depressed people deprive themselves of resourceful states for the purpose of keeping those states safe. They fear that, if someone powerful detects these states, forced loss will follow. In other words, they lock themselves in the money-filled safe to watch over and protect the money. But you cannot spend any of the money while locked in the safe with it. For safety's sake such people protect all their believed valuable and vulnerable states by refusing to access or utilize them. Unfortunately, the only felt loss happens within self. They lock themselves up with their states, but then can't use any of them in their environment.

Depressed people deprive themselves of resourceful states for the purpose of keeping those states safe.

In the metaphor that follows, we will look at the general dynamics of paranoia, how it comes to life and then spirals to an ever-widening sphere of influence. The expanding influence follows the principles of "if some is good more is better".

The principle within the story reveals the process found in creating a state of paranoia. The metaphor will also illustrate the more general principles found in most dysfunctional thinking and behavior. As we have seen, a state of equilibrium acts as the natural central operating position for people until adversity occurs when they are occupying the state. If this circumstance happens early enough in life, it may be of sufficient impact that a person chooses to vacate the state and its associated resources.

Generally, the later in life the adversity the less likely it will outweigh the accumulated history of safety felt with the original state. People may then remain in the equilibrium state and utilize its resources for solutions. People may also find solutions in other states but the state corresponding to the unpleasant occurrence is not deemed off-limits.

For a traumatic event in adult life to dislodge a person from equilibrium, it usually requires a serious emotional trauma. Since abandoning the state associated with the unpleasant event works supposedly to stop future adversity, then the person will move only one notch away from the point of equilibrium. If the aversive event continues or recurs, then she believes these modified states are also to blame for the trauma. In response to this, she then moves further away from the state associated with the "problem". These additional moves may result in her creating maladaptive Meta-States^R or a broad collection of primary states that feel uncomfortable to use.

The overzealous security guard

Our story illustrating paranoia concerns a security guard at a large manufacturing plant. The owner assigns the guard to overseeing the safety of the plant and its employees. This includes screening all people who want to enter the plant. Only one gate exists and this is in front of the plant. Each worker or potential visitor must pass through the guard's checkpoint. Because of the arrangement, the owner and all the employees feel safe and secure while at the plant. The workers can now focus solely on their tasks rather than wonder about possible problems or personally endangering situations brought on by unwelcome visitors.

All goes well until one day the security guard accidentally lets someone enter the plant who later causes problems for the plant's owner. Normally, no salespeople are permitted on the plant grounds without an appointment to call on the owner. However, in this case, a salesperson poses as a troubleshooter for one of the pieces of equipment used by the employees. Letting the "repair person" in seems like the solution to the problem. The impostor fits the description of a troubleshooter and the plant does need one at the time. But all is not as it appears to be.

The situation unfolds with the salesperson putting the owner on the spot by confronting him. Angrily, the owner tells the salesperson to leave the building. The security guard escorts him off the property. Once finished with the incident, the guard feels guilty for letting the boss down. He allowed someone to infiltrate his domain and go against his very purpose for being there.

Vowing never to let this happen again, he vigilantly assumes his post the next morning. Renewing his vigor, he closely observes each person asking for entry into the plant. This creates some delays for employees in getting into work and doing their jobs. In turn, this causes some drops in production for the plant as workers have slightly less time for actually performing their jobs. But the security guard remains determined to keep out the unwanted. Along with the new style, though, comes some distress for the guard. There is pressure to screen all potential entrants thoroughly, yet he is again getting feelings of incompetence because he is causing a different sort of problem for the company. They hired him to prevent problems and here he is creating them.

The guard becomes convinced that the solution to the problem is hiring another security guard. This would allow just as thorough processing, but at a faster rate. Now double diligence takes its post. In order to remember whom to keep out of the plant, the guards keep a photograph of the former interloper just for identification and prevention purposes.

Now, with a second security guard, our hero can afford to run things a little tighter. All those who want to enter the plant are now compared to the picture of the one-time offender. While increasing their vigilance by noticing current similarities to the original problem situation, the guards have forgotten their original positive intentions. (In theoretical terms, at lower levels of development we notice only outward indicators and ignore differences and intention. At lower levels of development we overgeneralize and jump to conclusions, using inductive logic. When this leads to more of the problem, we just increase the problem-making behavior. Some is good, but more is better.)

Now, even more elaborate screening procedures are used to scrutinize people passing through the checkpoint. If anyone resembling the impostor tries to gain entry, the guards quickly turn him away. Additionally, the guards allow no troubleshooters into the plant, no matter the need, because "once bad, always bad". However, this becomes a problem in itself as sometimes equipment breaks down needing troubleshooting and eventual repair.

The company's business declines at this point because no person claiming to be a troubleshooter, or anyone looking like the impostor, is allowed to pass through the gate. Even though the owner talks with the guards about their overzealous performance, they continue trying to fulfill their purpose in the same way. The plant is increasingly held hostage by the (supposedly protecting) security guards.

At one point an employee in the company's upper echelon leaves employment and begins working for a competitor. Various company inside knowledge is now carried to the competition. Considerable damage occurs to the original manufacturing plant's position in the business world. The security guards take this personally. They now have a second flaw in their record, according to their own perspective. They vow never to let anyone pass through the gates if they think that person might one day betray the company. From this point forward they will use photographs of both the imposter and the departing employee to determine who can and cannot pass through the gates.

Soon the guards turn away several people who physically resemble either the salesperson or the turncoat. This screening process in itself takes much longer than the original method. The result decreases production due to a smaller available workforce. When the company attempts hiring new employees, the prospects cannot even get past the gate for the interview. After all, how can the security guards trust them? They do not even work for the company. The plant continues its downward spiral. Each new decline in business strength leads the guards to tighten their grip that much more.

Gradually, fewer and fewer employees are permitted to come into work. The guards continue their policy of not allowing any people resembling the first two troublemakers to enter the plant. However, as the business withers away, each new decline serves as a reason for increasing the number and types of people not permitted entrance into the plant. First the guards just kept out two types of people but now they turn away six to eight physical types.

Then anyone wearing brown is denied entrance, and eventually anyone wearing brown, blue, or black cannot pass. Eventually the plant owner comes to work one day and he too is denied permission to enter the plant. The overzealous security guard puts himself out of work. This happened not because he employed such an effective system that he was no longer needed, but because he sealed off the plant from any and all input.

In real life, this thinking-perceiving style may be the point where psychosis sets in. All information in the environment is increasingly filtered to such an extent that it becomes the same and no new information is perceived. In the case of paranoia, all information is perceived as being dangerous. This limited perceptual style leads to noticing only surface similarities rather than any differences between stimuli.

The paranoid perceiver has an agenda of identifying the similarities between a formerly dangerous stimulus and a current stimulus. He feels compelled to find similarities or else he'll feel endangered because he cannot find the danger. When he does find the red herring he then feels endangered. If someone wearing red once hurt me then red is dangerous. Now the Pope visits wearing red so I assault him. Some would refer to this as delusional thinking. But this thinking is the consequence of generalizing taken to an extreme.

Levels of human development play a role in this delusional thinking style. Rigidity characterizes lower levels of human development. Overgeneralizing, or sorting information for similarities, spirals out of control. This severs the person from any novel input from the environment. A stimulus is considered new only if we notice how it differs from other stimuli rather than how it is similar.

The only way a person can tag new stimuli as just another example of the original is by ignoring the differences and looking for similarities.

The paranoid person then takes on a delusional thought process. These people live in a fantasy world made up of such a tightly woven fabric that reasoning with them seems nearly impossible. They distort all stimuli to fit their pre-existing beliefs. Even the act of attempting to reason with this person results in your becoming convicted as one of the "untrustworthy". You are perceived as trying to take away their "safety shield". Paranoia also enters the scene because a state (for example, assertive expression of self) is missing. Paranoia wonders who took the state and what other states someone might try to take.

The process of overgeneralizing seems to play one of the most influential roles in creating many significant "symptoms" or "diagnoses". Essentially, an individual experiences an emotional trauma or a series of similar traumas and then generalizes from them in his future. He looks for cues in the present circumstance that resembles the past traumatic circumstance. He then responds in the present the same way he did in the past. If he repeats this overgeneralizing enough and it results in behavioral or emotional trouble, he receives a diagnosis.

Diagnoses might be more useful if they addressed the way overgeneralizing is applied rather than its by-products, such as paranoia, anxiety, depression. The specific result of the overgeneralizing, the diagnosis, does not represent the "problem" but the endpoint of the generalizing process. It would be more helpful in assisting change to identify the process used in creating the unpleasant outcome. This problem-producing process is actually just a series of perceptual styles or selective attending. Changing the process will yield the solution.

Maybe it would be of some use diagnosing along the lines of "overgeneralizing syndrome as applied to—" and just fill in the blank. For example, generalizing "as applied to mistrust of others" (paranoia) or "as applied to danger in environmental interaction", as is the case with agoraphobia. This approach could also produce diagnoses such as "overgeneralizing syndrome"—as applied to potentially dangerous stimuli", as is the process for panic and anxiety disorders.

Many of the disorders found in the DSM-IV (American Psychiatric Association, 1994) have things in common. Bear in mind that "successful" overgeneralizing predicates itself on sorting for similarities in the environment. Sorting for how stimuli differ from the original (threatening) one short-circuits the overgeneralizing process. As a result, if the situation is not what we thought it was, we are now free to decide what it is. Seeking similarities in our surroundings only maintains a trance, while sorting for how things differ breaks a trance state.

Chapter Nine
The Dynamics and Consequences of Assertiveness and its Variations

Now we will focus on the concept and applications of assertiveness. This state of assertiveness and its variations seem to play a crucial role in our ability to access and utilize states of equilibrium.

We begin with a look into what is known as obsessive-compulsive disorder (OCD). This diagnostic category refers to repetitive or ritualistic thoughts and/or behaviors. Notice the diagnosis has a key word at the end—"disorder". Do realize that we each tend to display some degree of obsessive-compulsive thought or behavior. For the obsessing or compulsive elements to become a disorder they must be a problem for the individual and interfere with effective living.

The overgeneralizing process described in the last chapter also appears in such syndromes as OCD, which stems from a drive to feel safe in the face of perceived threats. A person believes she has no control over these threats. This drive for safety seeks equilibrium by compensating with alternative behaviors. The drive seems to result when the state of "assertive self-expression" is considered inappropriate in response to differences of opinion or interpersonal conflict.

Assertiveness could provide sought-after safety, but those utilizing an OCD style believe it is unsafe to assert themselves. In the past, assertive behavior met with overpowering response from a significant other. With assertiveness now unavailable as a response option, only passivity or aggression are available. Passivity seems to win out as a choice most of the time.

As a result, the other one must manage the suppressed anger that could be used more effectively in asserting oneself. A person must gain a feeling of safety without expressing her true emotions. This is quite a tall order. As a result, people with OCD compensate by generating order and symmetry in their environment. This seems to act as an emotional resetting device, discharging emotions temporarily through some substitute means.

The person using OCD may count certain items, arrange them in a particular way, or go through some ritualistic steps as they pursue safety and eventual calm.

This does not work for any significant length of time so she must repeat the process often. The unusual specifics found in each individual case may result from simple associating at the time of adverse events. While OCD is a freestanding disorder and not a personality disorder *per se*, it accompanies most, if not all, personality-disordering processes. It acts as a stabilizer for the otherwise out-of-balance states, dispensing much pent-up tension through the OCD rituals. I find borderline, narcissistic, histrionic, paranoid, and the other types of disordering usually include some degree of the OCD style.

The role of assertiveness in this process acts as a meta-state and is perhaps a perceptual filter as well. After all, assertiveness is also a manner of sorting within self. If you allow yourself assertive expression, then you select your self-expression accordingly. Regardless, assertiveness acts as a vehicle and a manner of expression, as do passivity and aggression. This vehicle known as assertiveness permits a free flow of self-expression without diversion. Providing additional influence to the flow is one's values system.

A SEE during childhood can interrupt this natural flow. A child may find herself in a situation calling for a state of assertive self-expression. It seems most likely that this state relates to expressing individuality, including differences of opinion with the powers that be. But the overpowering significant other forbids this assertive expression of individual differences. The differences and urge to express do not disappear. Rather, they go underground and shunt self expression.

The process of OCD goes in a downward spiral of thinking and feeling. Based on what clients have told me in counseling, self-doubt seems to be a catalyst for the vicious circle. This state of doubt originates because these people doubt self instead of assertively self-expressing. In essence, they doubt their self, thoughts, feelings, and behavioral wants. Not doubting, but self-expressing instead, puts them in direct opposition to the powers that be. The doubt seems to lead to something akin to self-contempt leading to self-worth erosion, followed by anger, sadness (grief over loss of the state known as "assertive self-expression"), and questioning of whether to exist at all. Coping with or diffusing these greatly distressing states leads to various behavioral and cognitive compensating devises. Hence, compulsive and obsessive cycles.

One particular client with OCD came to realize that his self-doubt really sought a state known as "fully alive". For him this meant fully and freely engaging in life. I asked him what he thought the opposite of doubt was and he answered "certainty". I then told him, "We know that doubt does not lead to being 'fully alive'; therefore, anything less than total certainty will not result in being 'fully alive'. " Realizing this concept promoted some significant shifting in his beliefs.

He continued referring to the state of doubt by gesturing to a place off to his lower right. So I asked him what his doubt needed. He said his doubt needed to know it was OK to doubt. Insightfully, he noted that he was the only one who could give his doubt the OK. I asked, "What will happen when you tell doubt it is OK?" He went on to describe how the state of doubt would feel that it was OK and not bad. This would change for the better how it thought, felt, and acted. I then suggested he could now tell his doubt that it is OK. He did so and immediately moved his eyes upward as though following a moving object. Doubt, the state, then took its place at the site of his already established ultimate meta-state at the top center of his visual field.

Doubt had transformed. I asked what became of doubt and how it would now conduct itself. After a brief search within he said it would now self-express. He seemed rather surprised by the simple yet logical shift to a more effective means of operating. I also asked how this resource would now contribute toward fulfilling his ultimate purpose, which led to more future-pacing.

He described his new goal of just expressing himself to others, instead of trying to gauge the response of the other party, as was the old goal. It was just important to get the information out on the table for discussion. This fits assertive self-expressing, which makes up the antidote or missing ingredient for rectifying OCD. However, all the assertiveness training in the world would not have given doubt the approval it needed and thus would have gone for naught. If the underlying belief about utilizing a state does not change, no amount of skill at using the state will matter.

Anger and OCD

Anger, to some degree, may be the state that drives a person to express differences of opinion. At least during childhood, people most often operate from the primary state of anger, or some variation of, when noting differences of opinion. If your initial effort at stating your difference of opinion gets ignored by the other person, what do you do next? Depending on values, most people either voice the opinion more forcefully or retract it.

It is important to note, though, that the way a person expresses the difference of opinion also depends on the developmental level from which she operates. If development progresses without a SEE, then a person may operate from higher-level Meta-States^R in response to differences of opinion. States such as "curiosity" about differences followed by "cooperation" may appear at higher levels of development. It seems likely that the SEE driving all-or-nothing thinking that is related to expressing anger (either keep anger in or let it all out in a fury) occurs during Loevinger's (1976) self-protective stage or maybe the conformist level. In Piaget's (1995) theory this would happen before age eight, when children's cognitive development limits them to all-or-nothing thinking. In Erikson's (1963) scheme the clog appears during the self-initiative-versus-guilt stage or about ages three to six.

People essentially freeze the injured part or state at the level of development when the injury occurs.

The term "arrested development" applies here. Developing additional self-expression skills (assertiveness training for example) would feel endangering. So the best a person can do is develop more elaborate ways of expressing passivity or aggression. She continues operating from the arrested developmental level in each instance of expressing differences of opinion. Keep in mind that the fear of expressing differences increases with the more authority or power the other person possesses.

In the face of childhood adversity, the state of assertiveness applied to anger or difference of opinion, or actually any state, goes underground. It resurfaces in a believed safer version known as passivity or aggression. This person now brings passivity to bear on expressing differences of opinion. Assertive expression is off-limits. However, the water continues to put pressure on the dam wall for its free flow. The ongoing stress occasionally results in aggressive outbursts. The continually accumulating water floods out over the top of the dam or bursts through a weak spot. In the course of day-to-day life, differences of opinion naturally occur. Suppressing these felt differences and conforming to others' ways only leads to an eventual anger overflow. When the amount of suppressed self (water) exceeds the limit of storage (dam), the person finds it very hard to control anger, often losing his temper.

Those with an OCD style commit their worst fear, even worse than assertiveness. They aggressively express their differences of opinion. More often than not, the person with OCD exerts just enough self-control for directing this anger overflow toward objects or the self. This process may reflect Loevinger's (1976) conformist level of development. The thinking may go something like this: "It is wrong to take my anger out on other people because they will probably disapprove and may then reject me. I'll aim my undeniable anger at myself or some inanimate object for safer discharge."

**More often than not, the person with OCD exerts
just enough self-control to direct this anger overflow
toward objects or self.**

This same person will usually admit to significant anger at himself. He feels angry about choosing to keep his feelings within himself. He may express this anger toward some object by smashing it or may verbally and even physically assault himself. Guilt and efforts at reinforcing the dam follow. The pressure only increases, setting the stage for another inevitable outburst. And so the cycle continues. Persons with OCD often receive the label "passive-aggressive", but this relates to the oscillating process of self-expression rather than the true disordering of personality. The personality-disordering style of passive-aggressive revolves around verifying personal freedom of choice, while the OCD-style person has safety as his goal.

The person experiencing OCD while believing that the passive expression of individual differences of opinion will provide safety proceeds in this style. But the actual outcome does not live up to the hope. The method of reaching a successful "solution" becomes the problem while the opposite style, self-expressing, represents the actual solution.

Assertiveness training often comes as standard equipment in the treatment of OCD. But it also often ends up as time misspent. If the state of assertiveness invokes fear, then all the training in the world in how to assert oneself will not overcome an assertiveness phobia. (To take an analogy, showing someone how to fold and pack a parachute and pull the ripcord as part of the pre-jump training on the ground goes by the wayside if the student's fear of heights prevents him from ever getting up in the air.)
People with OCD often keep themselves from assertive behavior because they believe it is bad. This comes about as a result of experiencing some form of rejection during a SEE in childhood. This fear must be overcome before assertiveness will happen. Until then, the OCD-style person will still believe that asserting herself is not OK.

**Assertiveness training often comes as standard treatment of
OCD. But it also often ends up as time misspent.**

How do people with OCD often carry symptoms of depression in addition to the disorder itself? It seems to happen because they feel a sense of loss and grief over the believed death of the state known as "assertive self-expression". Further, what makes for the intrusive thoughts that people with OCD report, the obsessive component? The intrusive thoughts may at times run counter to the individual's core values. Awareness of these thoughts sends streams of anxiety and distress through the person.

The discordant thoughts may occur because they represent the only other response option to passivity. If assertiveness is taboo and passivity only leads to frustration, then the only other known response is aggression. The person realizes that passive behavior does not work very well, though sometimes this is the chosen response, repetitive passive diversions. The only known potential alternative is aggression. This option generates more concern and fear than the ineffective, but at least self-detrimental, state of passivity. The aggression option hurts others and brings in the risk of rejection.

We can account for the obsessive elements in much the same manner as the compulsive behavior. The purpose of the obsessing is to generate some temporary safety.

The moderating variable in this process of imbalance is the compulsive element. Performing certain tasks in just certain ways permits some sense of balance in people's lives. The result keeps internal and external conflicts at bay, allowing a sense of safety for a short time, but the lack of any solution as a result of the compensating behavior means that its frequent repetition is necessary. We can account for the obsessive elements in much the same manner as with the compulsive ones. The purpose of the obsessing is to search for and generate some temporary state of safety, though the process usually generates anxiety. This developing anxiety then leads to its discharge through compulsive behaviors. All the while, the true state that leads to safety—assertiveness—remains out of bounds.

Some of the thoughts and impulses associated with OCD reveal the shadow side of the individual. If passivity is the chosen response to the unavailability of assertiveness, then aggressiveness becomes the only other response option. Aggressiveness is then considered even worse than the assertiveness that's bad. Since aggression is the only possible alternative to passivity, aggressive response options intrude into the person's mind. The OCD person restricts himself to a narrow range of thought and behavior all in line with general passivity. This sets the stage for onslaughts of aggressive impulses. Notice the dichotomized, all-or-nothing thinking, the trademark of disequilibrium.

The OCD serves the purpose of attempting to keep dangerous impulses at bay. Once again the symptom or diagnosis is not the problem, but is the best compensating attempt when equilibrium is unavailable. The thinking in OCD may include violent thoughts or thought wildly at odds with a person's core values. If she's religious, maybe while sitting in church she has blasphemous thoughts intruding into her mind. This only escalates her anxiety.

At times people do succumb to their unwanted impulses and display a burst of verbal or physical violence. They usually direct their violence toward objects or, very often, the self. The latter includes great self-criticism. This outburst unleashes cascading guilt, self-recriminating internal dialogue, and possible depression. They vow never to permit this to happen again. The noose only tightens.

Keep in mind that the person suffering from an OCD is different from the one suffering a "passive-aggressive" personality disorder. While displaying some common behaviors, they operate from different planes. As we saw in Chapter 7, departing from equilibrium makes bipolar beings of us all. We move from one end of the continuum to the other, "leap-frogging" the midrange.

While the OCD style operates on the passive-aggressive plane in search of safety, it differs from the passive-aggressive personality.

Passive-aggressive personalities operate on the freedom-seeking continuum using passivity or aggressiveness as a means of preserving freedom. They also utilize degrees of choosing (choosing constantly or refusing to choose) as a means of protecting their freedom. The OCD person displays passive and aggressive behaviors as a coping mechanism while self-expression remaining off-limits. The true passive-aggressive personality finds solace in his or her behavior, while the OCD person finds only distress.

Case study

In our first session, Amanda presented as experiencing depression. After we explored more we also found a process known as *intermittent explosive disorder*. This disorder is characterized as generally calm behavior punctuated by occasional verbal aggression or physically violent outbursts.

In Amanda's case, the outbursts were directed toward self or objects. She might launch into an internal dialogue, berating herself after some minor social mistake. At times Amanda might experience such rage over a mistake she made that she would go home and break some item she owned. After I had collected more information about her thought–emotion–behavior triad, a well-developed OCD was revealed. She would internally count items repeatedly and arrange certain items in ritualistic patterns. It consumed much time and frustrated her greatly. Within the world of psychiatry, Amanda officially qualified for four diagnoses. These were depression, intermittent explosive disorder, depression, and obsessive-compulsive disorder.

Examining the pieces that made up Amanda's mental structure, we found that the central missing state was assertive self-expression.

She felt a great need to comply always with socially expected behavior and not make waves. At the same time she could experience the natural and healthy of anger. Because Amanda could not make waves and could not display assertiveness, she could direct her anger only toward herself for not adequately complying with the rigid established structure. She utilized external standards (other people) rather than internal.

Using other people to decide whether she could express, Amanda felt disconnected from the resource state she needed to interact successfully with her environment. Assertiveness being off-limits, access to desired opportunities was essentially blocked. Depression came into being. Depression seems to be a belief that we do not and cannot have the resources we want or need within us. For Amanda, the equilibrium state of assertiveness was as good as dead.

Therapy targeted the process and purpose of the states that were not resourceful. She described depression as a hole into which she went for hiding and eventual problem solving. We noted that the only way she could implement the potential solutions was exiting depression in order to interact with her environment. We then simply adjusted her envisioned depth of the hole (depression) so it would function more in line with her purpose for it. The visual adjustment left depression as just a small indention in an otherwise level plane. She could use this place for pausing and contemplating (internal search for resources) rather than become stuck in it.

The second session focused on her considerable suppressed anger. Linguistics served as a loosening devise on the tight belief "bolts" supporting the anger structure. We identified and utilized the intended purpose of her behavior versus the behavior she actually displayed. For example, she intended to act in a peaceful or calm way. But when it came to her behavior she actually behaved in an aggressive, destructive way. The resulting discrepancy between intention and actual behavior provides leverage for adjusting and fine-tuning the structure.

Essentially the discrepancy between intention and actual behavior amounts to cognitive dissonance (Festinger, 1957). The dissonance motivates a person to bring the behavior in line with the original intention. This process brought modification to the anger and set the table for final alignment. Amanda's anger responses, which had been impulsive, became more conscious. She could then modify them into more constructive responses and gain the self-control she also desired.

Cognitive dissonance motivates a person to bring behavior in line with original intention.

The third and final session blended the remaining aggressive impulses and associated anger with the passive-compliance parts. This process brought the client back to her original state of equilibrium—in this case it was assertiveness. She now operated from the midrange of thoughts, feelings, and behaviors within the state of assertiveness. Depression vanished fully, including the former residual indentation.

No longer did Amanda need explosive outbursts, since modifying the state of anger became possible. The other influence of returning to the state of equilibrium was that the OCD no longer served any purpose. She released it fully. There were no emotions or impulses to keep at bay. These three sessions each used linguistic loosening and visual integrating methods. The client reported that she no longer needed to pretend she was happy. She used to act the part in the past. She now actually experienced happiness (associated into the state).

By the time a client enters a therapist's office, the tip of the iceberg can appear quite misleading. Traditional psychology states that people with personality disorders lack the ability to learn and adjust from experience. In some ways we don't give enough credit to these people for their learning abilities. The personality-disordered have learned quite well and very quickly, at an age when children may get little credit for their complex learning ability. Their early childhood experiences were so full of learning opportunities that were retained so well, that new experiences rarely amounted to enough to outweigh the earlier ones.

Early painful experiences were of such magnitude that the child perceived them as life-threatening. The forming of these early beliefs served to guide the child away from regular or effective use of self. In fact, personality-disordered people do believe they are utilizing self in the safest most effective way possible. Personality-disordered people do learn. They learn what they consider the most important lesson in life: survival. Everything else pales in comparison.

Rectifying the disordering process requires getting beyond the existing guard, in this case a belief that self-destruction will happen if the self is utilized.

The result is that such people will not even show the belief to others lest they endanger the belief and, ultimately, the self.

Showing the doctor where it hurts seems a forbidden act. If it is examined it might be healed and then the time bomb (access to and operating from self) detonates.

Extreme cases of personality disordering may lead to psychosis. The thought processes of psychosis are so far removed from the self and its resources, developing so many perceptual filters, that a person perceives a reality separate from what most of us perceive. So much of what occurs, both inside the individual and in the environment, must be filtered out to maintain a safe self-image.

All perceiving must feed the drive for a self-protection. People can perceive neither the internal imprisoning of self nor the external expressing of self. Deletion of stimuli runs rampant. This results in a significant distortion of "reality" and construction of a safe one that maintains the necessary awareness, or lack thereof, for safety. Psychotics may actually be walking the plank but behave as though they were walking on a quiet beach, or vice versa. Perceiving more of reality invokes full anxiety and depression states, so they must keep reality at bay.

The next chapter deals with methods of intervening, including specific meta-stating and other forms of inducing functioning at a higher developmental level. These apply to any and all diagnoses or maladaptive coping mechanisms. We will then compare the various Meta-States^R to the different levels of human development, finding a parallel. Ultimately Meta-States^R comprise the levels of human development. Access to and use of these higher levels of development, or Meta-States^R, is available immediately and continuously except in the cases of personality disordering.

While all states remain available to everyone, personality-disordered people cannot permit themselves access to the higher states of functioning. A much slower and more prolonged effort is required to resolve these restrictions to self. Other diagnoses have unfettered access to evolving beyond their state of dysfunction and operating from a higher plane. Depending on the complexity or number of states involved, remedies in the form of general meta-stating provide quick, thorough, and effective solutions. We now move to viewing ways of promoting higher human functioning through therapeutic techniques.

Chapter Ten
The State of the Slate: The Emancipating Proclamation

Maladaptive behaviors spring from either anxiety or depression. We either fear associating into a needed state or mourn the belief that we cannot do so. With these two roots of distress identified, intervention techniques then address the dynamics of anxiety and/or depression. Within therapy itself, it seems that common to all effective therapy is the general process of meta-stating, identified by Hall (1995, 2000). That may seem a big claim, but meta-stating is common to all effective change-making interventions because central to personal change is a change of state.

All effective therapeutic techniques rely on the general process of meta-stating identified by Hall.

Each state that functions meta to a lower one carries with it increased awareness. This increased awareness removes more perceptual blinders, permitting new choices and invoking additional resources. Regardless of the theoretical orientation of the intervention, each effective method involves meta-stating the client. The difference between the interventions is how the meta-state is reached—behaviorally, cognitively, emotionally, or experientially.

Meta-stating is like climbing an observation tower. Each successive step lets you see and know more, which results in a greater awareness. A hallmark of human developmental theories is that each successive level of development endows the person with expanded awareness. So we find that meta-stating a person directly elevates the person's level of human development, allowing positive change in thought, emotion, and behavior.

Our wellbeing results from our relationship with our states. Two basic positions exist in relation to our states. We either associate into a state, like the clothes you are now wearing, or we dissociate from a state. This dissociated relationship is like the clothes available to you in your closet that you are not wearing right now. The two central criteria for entering or associating into any state are its safety and availability. Perceiving both, not just either separately, permits access to and entry into the state. The safety issue addresses anxiety while the availability factor pertains to depression.

Two particular consequences happen as the result of a SEE. We bind to a limiting state and restrict ourselves from a resource state.

The state we bond to becomes the supposed "safe" state that defends the remainder of the organism—a defense mechanism. The states we restrict ourselves from are associated with the SEE. The restricted states are the those we occupied at the time of the adverse event. Because of unconscious, almost instinctive, associating of cause and effect (transductive logic), we attribute the adverse event to the state. The result is that we avoid the state we were utilizing at the time of the adversity and take "refuge" in some fear-based state.

Remaining associated into the state we were in at the time of the adversity, or going meta to it, supplies the resources needed for solving the problem. The problem scenario is external to us, not within us. It is not the fault of the state. If we do not keep or access the resourceful state, then the fear-based state takes over. The fear-based state determines our way of thinking and behaving, bringing with it a whole host of other troubles, which create the real problem from that point forward. The outcome is a self-fulfilling prophecy of an unwanted kind.

In their simplest form, emotional and mental problems are the result of an illusion that some resource state poses a danger to us.

This illusion sets in motion many compensating efforts that constitute the problem. We spend much of our lives compensating for an illusion!

Consider an athlete who is injured while practising. She had been in a state that allowed her to use her physical skills to the fullest. We might call this "trust" of physical self. Once injured, she goes into a self-limiting state of anxiety, fearful of trusting and utilizing her physical skills. She clings to fear while holding herself back from her strengths. What she does not realize is that her strengths were not the problem and in fact hold the solution. At most, some slight adjustment of her physical skills will bring the solution.

The whole skill set is not the problem (overgeneralizing). Just one minor adjustment will solve this. But her illusion that the state of trust made her vulnerable leads her to compensate with a self-limiting state. After this shift away from trust, she then needs to compensate for what are now the aftereffects of not trusting herself. The problem comes from the compensating state.

> **Perception determines what information we have available to consider. By altering perception we can remove barriers to states.**

Given the general problem, how can we verify safety and availability of internal resources? Perception determines what information we have available to consider. By altering perception we can remove barriers to states. The meaning we attribute to any perceived event shapes our response. One way to alter the meaning of a situation comes in the explanation below.

Translating fear's message

We now deal with fear and the role it plays in our lives. More importantly, this section of the chapter translates fear's message, converting it into a message that fulfills its true intention. The first assertion presented here is that fear is about what *might* happen instead what *is* happening. Even during an event that scares us, the fear springs from what could happen if the situation progressed beyond its current status. I believe fear never concerns itself with the here and now but with what the here and now might become.

Fear is a lookout that scans the horizon for the worst possible scenario. But the purpose of the scanning is so we can avoid the event. By a cognitive glitch of literal translating we actually end up moving toward our most feared outcome. If you were hiking through the woods and suddenly came upon a bear, you would most likely experience fear. This fear thrives on what could happen rather than what is currently happening.

Fear takes a slippery and elusive form. For its survival, fear must remain at least one step ahead of the present. Living in the present, imagining only solutions to any challenge, makes fear disappear. Fear simply cannot exist when we look into our future for solutions while gazing from the present. Your future does not know your past.

Learning to accurately interpret the real message of fear can make fear into an ally.

There was a device that used to be on many vehicles a few decades ago. They were called curb feelers. This thin, flexible, metallic, spokelike probe extended about 10–12 inches (25–30 centimeters) out from each side of the vehicle, near the tires.

Usually the vehicle had four of these curb feelers, sometimes just two. These devises helped the driver when parking next to the curb. When the car got close to the curb, the feeler would scrape the concrete, making a noise and causing some vibration that could be felt through the steering wheel. This would signal the driver that he had moved too close to the curb.

Fear, and in fact all emotions, attempt to provide us with vital information—just as the curb feeler did. However, the language of emotions limits them, leaving the translating up to us. Our traditional style of interpreting language often involves communicating about what to do rather than what not to do. So, when fear communicates to us, we naturally assume it asks that we look more closely at the fear. Doing this we find only more fear. We then assume it again asks that we look still more closely. The power of the microscope increases. Now our fear really escalates.

This ever-spiraling process of fear predicates itself on our misunderstanding the message from fear. Fear serves as a curb feeler, telling us we have just made contact with the curb. It then informs us we need to right ourselves away from the curb. Fear is feedback from our future that tells us to take some sort of evasive action. This evasive action comes to us through our resourceful states, which can prescribe solution options.

Fear asks that we alter our course to a smoother path toward what we do want rather than what we do not want.

Investigating fear wastes our time. This process results in driving our vehicle up and over the curb. Rather, make good use of time investigating options for corrective action. Fear asks that we *do* this. Fear asks that we alter our course to a smoother path toward what we do want rather than what we do *not* want. Fear is an ally and a catalyst. It encourages us to change for the better. We may welcome the first inkling of fear, translating it into adaptive change for the better. It asks only that we do what we really want to do all along. Let yourself become aware of your fear and then find its true message. Then take immediate action and notice how fear disappears.

You may doubt this inverse correlation between fear and action. Notice how fear increases the more we focus on it while not choosing a different course of action. Also notice how fear decreases in proportion to the degree that we take constructive, fulfilling action. In essence, you get more of whatever it is that you choose to make your focus. We possess exquisitely precise control over every minuscule increment of fear. We have always possessed this exquisitely precise control over fear, but we have used it in the manner opposite to that which fear asked us to adopt. Now notice the feeling you experience when you utilize your power by design. Suddenly, no fear, unless you want or need a gentle nudge or a reminder to correct the direction of your life.

Case study
Here is a specific example of changing perception and thus changing meaning. I worked with a client, Mark, who described a very negative self-image and resulting depression. Because of this

self-concept, he constantly remained on guard, looking for evidence to support his belief. When he inevitably found the evidence, no matter how much he had to delete and distort, the "red herring" then activated a self-protecting response.

Mark attended a local university. He told me in our counseling session about an event that took place several months before I knew him. Mark was in an accounting class on the first day of the semester. The professor in this class had also taught him in a class last semester. On the first day in this semester, the professor told a story about one of the major accounting firms in the nation looking for only pretty faces to hire, rather than emphasizing skill level.

The client, already believing he was unattractive, assumed the story was about him (egocentric) and how he should just get out of class now. Mark thought the professor singled him out, telling him in particular. It was all Mark could do to drag himself into the next class. He really just wanted to drop the class. All he felt was great anxiety and even more social discomfort.

In our session, I asked what evidence Mark could offer that supported his belief that the professor's story was directed at him. He could not come up with anything other than feeling driven by his preconceived beliefs about himself. I asked Mark what else the story might be saying. He had no idea, so I suggested an alternative point of view. I offered that the story might actually be slighting the values of the major accounting firm for its superficial approach to hiring.

By describing the firm's criteria, we showed that the story related to the firm and not to Mark. This being the case, how did Mark now interpret the professor's story? Also, maybe the professor's intention was to provide helpful hints about where not to apply for work, saying that skills can count for something important beyond one's looks.

Mark admitted he did not think in this selfless way about the professor's story. Once he did this he realized the professor was actually helping him. In fact, it turned out that the next story the

professor told the class related to the differences between accounting firms and being on the lookout for one with values similar to
one's own. But, from Mark's previous self-condemning belief,
he'd forgotten all about the story in the next class. Now the stories
became positive and supporting to the client's future. Future
pacing with the new perspective found him not wanting to
drop classes.

**By changing how we interpret information, we can change
what we find. We can then find the safe availability of a state.**

Mark developed an ability to interpret information more effectively so he could respond in ways consistent with meeting his
goals. Now he can generalize this new perceiving skill, finding
more useful information. By changing how we interpret information we change what we find. Remember searching for only
the color blue? To search for this you must ignore the other
colors in the spectrum. Once you change the target of the search,
you become aware of new colors. This new awareness can then
help you find the safety a state. The desired state he believed
unavailable to him was something such as "self-acceptance".
Once he found and reclaimed the "lost" state, his depression
vanished.

Let us look now at depression. This condition stems from abandoning a desired resource state. This abandonment happens
because the individual comes to believe the state is dangerous to
her. The desired state is now unavailable and she grieves this loss.
This process is the essence of depression.

The abandoned state once existed in a neutral or positive way.
After a SEE the resource state came to be seen as threatening to the
person because the state got the blame for the SEE. Doing away
with the state became essential for survival. And, while the state is
not really done away with, it is made dormant.

**You can't update a state if it continues its dormancy,
removed from the light of day.**

But one particular problem comes along after the person rejects a
state. She never takes another look at the conditions around her to

find out if the state can be safely used again. Not checking to determine if the "dangerous" conditions remain sustains the problem. Also, there exists no chance for new awareness to enter. You can't update a state if it continues its dormancy, removed from the light of day. No updating of awareness occurs if the state is not brought into the light of day to interact with the environment. The following analogy illustrates this process of compensating for and reviving abandoned states.

After the war

How do you now know when conditions around you are safe? The consequences of answering this question hold immense transformational power. If a person believes conditions endanger a valuable resource, then he tends to hide the resource to preserve it. But, while hidden away, these resources remain inaccessible. The purpose of concealing the resource is to permit its future use. But how will the organism know when the danger has passed, making it safe to access these resources again? When do you open up a time capsule and how do you interpret the contents? What is the purpose of human cryogenics. And how do you know when to thaw the frozen one? How long should you wait after meeting the criteria and why? These questions lead us into an analogy that illustrates the importance of timing in hiding and accessing resources.

To answer the questions above, I'll use the example of the fairly long-running thirty-minute situation comedy *Hogan's Heroes*, which originally aired in the 1970s in the United States and was also shown on British television. It was set during World War II in a German concentration camp, where a group of Allied soldiers were held prisoner. These soldiers included an American colonel by the name of Hogan. He and a small group of prisoners worked together in various covert ways to provide assistance to the Allies fighting the Axis Powers.

The group of prisoners developed elaborate schemes for finding out enemy war plans and creatively communicated these to the Allies. They also sneaked out of camp and took part in the destruction of strategic enemy targets. The heroes managed to develop radio communication and bomb-making materials and made tunnels to get out of and back into the camp without being detected. These prisoners developed quite an elaborate and effective structure to compensate for their limitations.

Now my question is, what happens after the war ends? What if the prisoners, no longer being prisoners, continued acting in the same way as when the war was ongoing? They would limit their effectiveness as well appearing way out of place and out of touch in the bigger scheme of things. What used to be effective problem-solving methods would now prove limiting as the context changed. All other prisoners and Germans at the camp would have long since left. The dilapidating camp now would now stand in disarray from neglect. There is no use for it anymore. A once highly prized group of courageous men would now seem odd in their behavior, if not dangerous to the public.

In this what-if scenario, the goal or purpose of these prisoners has remained the same in spite of the changes in circumstances. They have continued working from an "as if it were still true" perspective about the war. Imagine all the weird behavior: sneaking in and out of camp through tunnels, attempting radio contact with the Allies, making bombs. This all because they lacked vital information (self-limiting due to beliefs) or did not apply the current information.

Naturalistic fallacy

Not staying in touch with current conditions, but rather viewing conditions through lenses made from childhood, makes us follow in the footsteps of the people in the example above. This process relates to a term known as naturalistic fallacy (Kohlberg, 1971). The concept involves identifying an ongoing process and converting it into a permanent status.

Naturalistic fallacy occurs by taking an "is" and making it a "should". The observer freezes an ongoing process.

Ignoring variance in the environment, reality "should" remain the same way as the time of the last observation. This happens if the person freezing the reality believes she has something to gain and/or lose by perceiving change. By what ways different from the past ways can these people become heroes again? If they do not keep up with the times they will eventually become antiheroes.

When an emotional trauma happens in childhood, the part of us that felt injured tends to remain developmentally delayed, living in the past. The solution for our younger part's issues resides in the future provided by our more developmentally advanced selves. What information or knowledge do our future selves have for our past selves that will provide the most needed solutions? Additionally, another factor involved in releasing the short leash of the past comes from recognizing the difference between the past and the present. What is and isn't now that was or wasn't then? The difference is the difference.

The following paragraph reads as a hypnotic language pattern, designed to increase and then shift awareness:

It remains so easy to perpetuate any behavioral style. Just look for the familiar similar cues and use them like pedals on a bike to keep the wheels going round and round. If we ever look at how a situation differs from what we believe, the drive chain comes off. But how do you look for and notice differences? You could compare even with odd but those terms just relate to numbers. You could note the difference between numbers and shapes. Yet you can see three triangles and you can square or cube a number. So how do we identify the differences rather than sort for sameness? After all, some might say it's impolite, pointing out the discrepancies. But sometimes it is essential for some programs to succeed. When is it imperative that you look for the way things differ? When you push but it's pull and you can't get in or out. Knowing when your birthday is and is not. When the light is green but you hesitate and doubt instead of going. Pouring on liquid for putting out the fire, but making sure to use water, not gas. Turning right gets you there while turning left gets you left out. Matching, but for opposites, not the same. Looking beyond the moment for antecedents before you got there. This may be one of those times for using the details you know—a new grouping. What do you get when you have what you didn't have before. Now look again at the new situation. What did you ignore before?

The character of Meta-States^R

Now let's look at states and Meta-States^R more closely to understand better their makeup and functioning. You could define states as states of mind or being. You could also consider states as adjectives for emotional states. For example, you may experience the states of curiosity, joy, optimism, acceptance, confusion, agitation, frustration, or peace from a collection of several hundred more. Within these states exists a collection of thoughts, feelings, and behaviors.

When you experience a state, this experience also generates an internal response. You may be in a state of confusion and then experience a state such as frustration about your confusion. But maybe you experience a state of motivation to understand, in response to your confusion. Remembering the difference between primary and Meta-States^R helps clarify between initial response states and our internal responses to these states. The term "primary states" refers to elements in our environment—things that are external to us or even physically felt within us.

You might think of primary states as being our initial response to information that comes to us through our five senses.

Maybe you experience the state of frustration when a friend does not show up for an arranged meeting. Our state concerns the other person's behavior and its perceived consequences.

Meta-States^R concern how we think or feel about our primary states or about other Meta-States^R. So we experience a primary state along with its thoughts, feelings, and behaviors. The meta-state stems from how we feel about utilizing the specific primary state. This includes how safe the state seems along with judgments about how well it works. Maybe we experience curiosity about our frustration. We may say to ourselves, "I don't know why I'm bothering to feel frustrated. My friend does this sort of thing all the time."

Meta-States^R refer to how we think or feel about our primary state or about other meta-states.

In this case, the meta-state of curiosity about frustration allows you to leave the state of frustration and move to some more resourceful state. There is also another layer of meta-state in the described process. The state of being bothered is meta to frustration while the state of curiosity is meta to being bothered. The assessment of thoughts-emotions takes you to a state that is meta to the primary one, what you think about your initial thoughts.

Meta-States[R] develop from our thinking about our own internal primary states or about other internal meta-states. Each successively higher meta-state takes precedence and rules over the ones below it. As a result we think, feel and behave out of the highest meta-state of which we are aware. Curiosity about bothering to feel frustrated may lead you to look for something else to do now that this planned event is not happening. This new perspective then opens up opportunities for experiencing satisfaction rather than frustration. Meta-stating is about this consciousness-raising process and increased resourcefulness that results. It parallels and shares significant characteristics with the levels of human development.

States as levels of human development

Just feeling the primary state of frustration may lead to impulsive-level (Loevinger, 1976) retaliatory responses. The state of "bothering to feel frustrated" may lead to self-protective-level responses. These responses may include such things as refusing to discuss with this person what happened to make him or her miss the get-together. When we "get over it" (shifting to a more resourceful and higher meta-state) we may then experience willingness to talk about what happened.

Meta-stating and the general personal freedom that results parallel and share many significant characteristics with the various levels of human development.

When we experience curiosity, we may bypass the responses of frustration and bother. If we bypass these states we can just go about the business of meeting our needs through available outlets instead of bothering to feel frustrated over unavailable outlets. This response set remains consistent with the conformist level of development. We could also go meta to curiosity and find a state such as comfort or calm. From this state we no longer concern ourselves with the missed meeting. We find that more important issues and causes take precedence.

An even bigger picture emerges when we shift to a state such as comfort or calm, which makes forgiveness moot. In the state of calm or comfort, nothing needs forgiving. We then get to have more of the feelings we really want and then choose responses from this position of awareness. This level of thought fits within Loevinger's conscientious level of development. At this level of development we may shift to hoping that nothing bad happened to the person who missed the lunch, wanting only to understand. The focus shifts from self to others and their welfare. At this conscientious level, personalizing other's behavior ceases. We may wish him or her well, yet continue on our path consistent with our clearer purpose.

Meta-stating this state of calm could lead to a state such as "utter peace" or "unity". This corresponds with Loevinger's autonomous level of development. Here we find bigger fish to fry and the missed meeting is no longer even a fish. We make our choices and act as we do because we *perceive from* heightened awareness, not so we will *get* heightened awareness. Higher levels of development such as the "integrated" level exist and higher meta levels exist, but these examples suffice for illustrating the principles at work. At these higher levels the fish and the frying pan disappear.

Revisiting Lawrence Kohlberg's (1969) theory of human development reveals the ways in which meta-stating prods development. Kohlberg determined that seven stages of moral development exist. He determines a person's level of moral development based on his or her reasons for his behavioral choices. Kohlberg's theory suggests that, as a person morally develops, she moves from self-absorption to other absorption to alignment with an abstract set of moral standards that are mutually exclusive of all people. While two people may behave in the same way, the same behavior may stem from very different reasons.

> **While two people may behave in the same way, the same behavior may stem from very different reasons.**

For example, a person may donate goods to charity. He may do this because of a desire to help those less fortunate. Another very different reason could be the donor's desire for glory and attention from others. The first person donated because doing so fits with high-level beliefs about helping improve others' quality of life. It is a selfless act. The second person draws motivation for donating from the praise he will receive for his "good" actions. The motivation stems from selfish needs.

Very different motivations can yield the very same behavior. Kohlberg would find the first person operating from his fifth, sixth, or even seventh level of development. The second person's behavior comes from one of the first two levels of behavior. Most likely it stems from the lowest levels: "What's in it for me?"

In Kohlberg's scheme the first six levels of development can be grouped into three categories of development, with the seventh level standing alone. The first group gives rise to behaviors revolving around the concern of how these actions will benefit the self. Regard for others is nonexistent. The second developmental category includes behaviors motivated by a "How can I please you?" attitude. This represents the essential opposite of the previous levels of moral development. However, this excludes the self, resulting in imbalance in the other direction. To this point the person struggled with either/or thinking in a broad way.

The third collection of moral reasoning derives its guiding force from universal principles. This may include justice, love, and general adherence to abstract principles encompassing the good of all rather than either/or. Operating from this level removes the opinions of other people as the first reference point in decision making. Rather, the individual using this third category of development will first consult the higher principles. He then gains insight and choice from them, applying his conclusions to the players in the situation.

Meta-stating in any form shifts people to a higher level of human development. During meta-stating, people move from a state of protecting self from the "dangers" of the environment (either of the first two clusters of development) to a state of abstract principles independent of the environment. From this position people tune in their higher-order thinking and reasoning and then view the situation at hand through this state. The result brings broader, more encompassing solutions with all parties considered. Leaving either side out of the solution would go counter to the higher-order principles.

Moving from an external to an internal locus of control is another result of meta-stating. First developed by Julian Rotter (1954), the locus-of-control concept refers to a person's belief about the source of control over his life. People with an external locus of control believe their lives are essentially controlled by factors in their environment. Hence, the external (to self) locus of control. They may feel helpless over their environment in effecting change in their lives.

People who utilize an internal locus of control believe the source of control over their lives resides within them.

People with an internal locus of control believe the source of control over their lives resides within them. They tend toward feelings of empowerment. Meta-stating people shifts them from believing the environment controls their life to awareness of and experience of their deepest internal resources for directing their own lives. They move from external locus to internal locus of control. Imagine the effect on perceiving the environment.

One way to determine the developmental level in action is to find out whether a person behaved a certain way in order to feel better or whether the behavior resulted from feeling good already. Actually, both are always true. We always seek higher meta-states. This relates to the NLP presupposition that behind every behavior there exists a positive intention. However, behaving a certain way in order to feel better reflects lower-level states attempting to self-elevate. Lower-level states cannot generate behavior beyond their level.

When a person states he behaved a certain way because "I just thought it might make me feel better", this almost always reflects behavior generated from lower-order or even primary states. We cannot behave beyond the state we operate from. If we could, we would then be in the advanced state. Behavior coming out of higher-order states results from our already feeling better because we occupy meta-state.

Behavior is always consistent with the level, meta or developmental, that gives it birth. For example, you cannot get the color yellow from the color blue, nor can you find foresight within an impulsive level of development. The state must change before the behavior can change. If a person attributes a behavioral choice to the environment, then it stems from a lower developmental level of thinking. If a person attributes behavior to adherence to abstract principles, this usually reflects higher-level development.

We can encourage or offer reinforcement to someone as incentive for going meta but the original behavior does not alter until the state does. At best, a person may mimic another person in order to receive the reward she noticed other people getting for their behavior. Behavioral psychology calls this modeling (Bandura, 1977). In the world of developmental psychology this process is known as pacing (D'Andrea, 1984). Ideally, the imitated behavior and subsequent rewards accumulate, helping the one who models gain a higher level of functioning or a higher level of meta-state.

People move up the "meta-ladder" and stay there because they experience the reward from occupying that level of thought.

If some is good, more is better, and we always and only change for a higher meta-level. People move up the "meta-ladder" and stay there because they experience the reward from occupying that level of thought. Initially they did not generate the advanced behavior: rather they just copied it. Before self-initiating higher-order behavior, the person must actually operate from this level. While this modeling or pacing method can affect positive change, meta-stating provides a more efficient and thorough change of thoughts, emotions, and behavior since it comes from within the person and not externally.

We can operate from a meta level or state that exists beyond our conscious awareness. We often do this. It takes the form of a sort of "auto-pilot." But in doing this we lose awareness of choice. The meta-state operates on its own agenda and we just act as passengers along for the ride. Meta-stating expands our awareness of the behavioral driving forces that had been out of conscious sight. Expanding our consciousness illuminates our higher states. This increased consciousness allows access and restores conscious choice.

Meta-stating expands our awareness of the behavioral driving forces that had been out of conscious sight.

If we do not access these driving Meta-States[R], yet endow the client with some increased meta-level functioning, the client just uses these expanded abilities for feeding and sustaining the original wound, instead of healing the SEE. Personality disorders employ this format. Here, the original wound calls the shots and all forces rally around for serving and protecting the state. The wounded state then never receives what it really needs (healing, thus setting it free from its moorings), and the protecting army just becomes stronger from the new resources it gobbles up. This vicious circle of "protectors" serves only to prevent any actual evolving, development, or meta-stating of the wounded state.

Meta-stating reverses the cause-effect belief that "problems" arise from the environment's influence on internal states.

What makes meta-stating effective as a means of healing? Meta-stating reverses the cause-effect belief that "problems" arise from the environment's influence on internal states, to a belief that states cause environmental conditions. Transductive logic and magical thinking seem to be a driving force in setting the stage for all believed "problems". Thinking with transductive logic attributes the power for influencing internal states to events going on around us. Magical thinking (Elkind, 1994) includes the faulty logic of children who believe they cause all events happening around them. It combines egocentricity with transductive logic.

The more emotionally powerful the event, the more likely we are to attribute to it the power for affecting our internal states. Endowing the environment with the power to cause our internal states sets up an adversarial relationship between our environment and ourselves. We now imagine our environment fraught with potential dangers. From this point forward, various defense mechanisms, perceptual filters, or meta-programs take positions for protecting us from our foe.

> **The more emotionally powerful the event, the more likely we are to attribute to it the power for affecting our internal state.**

Meta-stating restores the original internal state to us. This makes up the most powerful change-producing feature of meta-stating I know. From this point of awareness forward we remain forever emancipated from our environment as dictator of our states. It removes the hook to the environment, permitting internal state management.

As people use transductive logic to initiate certain acts in order to feel better, they attempt to steer their environment toward a desired outcome. This outcome will then supposedly cause a desired internal state for them. While this sometimes works effectively, it actually sets up a rather maniacal "slave to our environment" relationship. We believe our internal states are at the mercy of our surroundings.

Meta-stating reverses the order of events. Here we access and experience the desired state first. We can do this, for example, by simply imagining we have already achieved the desired external conditions. In the process of imagining this desired outcome, we then discover that the power for generating internal states resides within. Just by imagining our desired state we can associate into it. The awareness that you can determine your own states frees us from environmental slavery. This ability in itself vaults us up one or two developmental levels. Impulsive and self protective people believe the environment holds control over them. Their behavior consists largely of fighting back against the environment.

People functioning from the first two or three levels of development often make statements such as he or she made me feel X. They generally phrase their expressions as attributing cause of their state to the environment. In fact, developmental psychology suggests that treatment for these first two developmental levels should consist of altering the environment as a means of influencing their behavior (Swenson, 1980), and thus eventually altering a state. This environmental change may include helping the parents increase their parenting skills the better to influence the child's behavior.

For young children, adjusting the environment to promote change works well, as with behavior-modification techniques. For teens and adults, meta-stating techniques promote more and faster development. Even conformists grant the majority of power in their lives to the environment. Why else would they consume themselves with fitting in? They try to keep their environment from ostracizing them. Utilizing the principles of meta-stating allows us safe influence upon our environment.

We first experience the desired state, then discover a multitude of resources better suited to causing the desired event in the external world. Instead of having event cause state, we now arrange it so state causes event. More importantly, awareness of controlling our inner states returns to us. Freedom of choice presents itself. This position corresponds well with the conscientious through autonomous stages of development described by Loevinger (1976). As the name implies people can know state autonomy. Their states operate free from environmental control.

Defusing the mental landmines naturally follows. Mental landmines here are cues in the environment that trigger limiting states from old learning. Following this, the quality and quantity of perceiving increases as external circumstances no longer endanger them. Direct life-threatening events remain as the exceptions. Perceiving more fully becomes safe now and in fact more beneficial than the protective filtering in place before. The two universal meta-programs take over from here, promoting safe availability of internal states. Realize also that meta-stating one part or aspect of a person does not necessarily generalize to other lagging parts. Each may need individual attention and meta-stating.

Chapter Eleven
Other Traits and Applications of Meta-States[R]

Instinctively, we refer to Meta-States[R] in our everyday language. We naturally make statements such as "Don't sink to their level"; "I thought you were above that"; "I can overlook that"; "That is beneath you"; Rise above it"; "Get over it"; "Live up to it". The hierarchical order of Meta-States[R] and meta-stating is a natural order of ourselves and the universe. What does not exist in a hierarchical arrangement? When hierarchy does not naturally occur we impose it, such as with military ranks, governmental levels, wind speeds—the list goes on.

Each higher level of meta-thought holds power and control over those levels beneath. Additionally, we all seek higher levels of meta-functioning. This world spends billions of dollars for people and things that assist them to higher meta-levels. We pay this money to actors, musicians, authors, athletes, drug dealers, and anyone reminding us of possible experiences at higher levels of being.

Certain characteristics exist that are common to Meta-States[R]. The first operating principle about regards the rank order of power between the layers of states. The higher meta-state holds power over all other states below it. For example, if you feel good about getting angry at someone, then the good feeling dominates. Gregory Bateson (1972) identified the hierarchical structure of Meta-States[R].

The exception to this power hierarchy involves an injured state. The state that experiences a SEE calls the behavioral shots unless and until it receives healing by having instilled into it awareness of higher meta-states. Higher states provide healing solutions. Receiving the necessary antidote, the formerly injured state willingly turns control over to superior states. Take for example a person feeling a sense of sadness as his primary state. He then feels a sense of fear about his sadness. From this state (fear of sadness) he then behaves in a very limiting way.

The state that experiences the SEE calls the behavioral shots unless and until it receives healing.

After thinking further, he may find a sense of calmness about his fear of sadness. Now above and beyond this calmness he notices feeling comfortable, peaceful, or free. Suddenly, he steps into awareness of his freedom. Now, from a state freedom, how does he choose differently from the way he chose in his state of sadness or fear of sadness? He chooses from his state of freedom unless he moves back down the state structure stepping into one of the lower two states. We all always think, feel, and behave from the highest state. We may or may not consciously know this, but, once we have come to know and experience freedom, why would we choose to operate from sadness?

Sometimes unconscious decision making can happen because of some power behind the conscious scene. A meta-state in our unconscious mind can dictate to our lower states, requiring we operate from sadness. Past experience may have led to aversive feelings associated with freedom. In this case, then, to exercise freedom feels as if it endangers the individual. We may ascend the meta-state ladder going to higher and higher meta-levels unless an injured state exists at a certain height. We cannot rise above the injured state without consciously attending to the wound.

The injured meta-state puts a ceiling on further development until it experiences the freedom that healing brings. This happens because the state believes, and the organism as a whole believes, that the injured state must not be used, at risk of personal disaster. Restricting yourself in terms of states utilized (you may think of this as emotional constriction) is a subtle form of communicating by the individual. This emotional restricting or constricting may be the only way for the individual to call out for help. But, if we identify and step into meta-states beyond freedom, we find the necessary power to override the fear of freedom. Now we experience freedom by being free.

A state of equilibrium that is vacated because of a SEE recruits other states and perceptual filters for protection.

Now we move to the second principle about states. If multiple states are injured or "unavailable", each one needs treatment. The treatment administered to one will not automatically spill over into the other restricted states. As we have discussed, these "dangerous" states dictate our thoughts, feelings, and behaviors unless and until we go meta to them. A state of equilibrium vacated because of a SEE recruits other states and perceptual filters for protection. These recruited states also need to be addressed in treatment. Once a resourceful meta-state overrides the wound, the states that supported the wounded state need also to experience this new resource state.

Recall the story about the man who wouldn't let himself experience happiness. The person who fears happiness sets in motion many defenses to keep him from experiencing the dreaded state. The organism must avoid using or operating from these dangerous states lest it risk becoming extinct. As a result the person may sabotage a situation that might have led to happiness. The anxiety alarm will go off when this person reaches a state that is just one step away from happiness. If you treat just anxiety, then he still can't reach happiness, since he believes happiness to be "dangerous" to him.

The third principle, then, is that just because we go meta to one state, find desired resources and apply them, this does not mean all other states in need of healing now automatically experience this resource. Yes, a meta-state modifies the states "under" it, but these lower states benefit more by having the healing resource state directly applied, and other limiting state constellations don't gain the benefits experienced by the one constellation that was effectively treated. Each state and each constellation needs to experience the healing resource meta-state directly.

Apparently, states resulting from an emotional trauma form a sort of constellation made up of a core state and those states recruited to protect the core. The protecting defense states form a sort of buffer around the core state. Each member of the constellation needs treatment because changing one member of the constellation does not necessarily change the others. For example, think about a woman who feels inferior to others. In response to these inferiority feelings, she feels disgust (meta-state) about her inferiority. This woman then feels anger (meta-meta-state) about her disgust and ultimately, sadness. In response to her sadness, the highest meta-state, she withdraws from others.

Looking further at the woman who withdraws, if treatment only involves the state of inferiority and/or the withdrawal behavior, you will not get significant influence on her disgust, anger or her sadness. The root-state must be addressed, sadness in this case, to best affect the whole system of states and behavior. Remember that the last meta-state in the chain is the highest state and rules those below. The state of withdrawal was recruited only as a defense mechanism. The belief system stemming from sadness goes something like, "I should not interact with other people because I'm no good and will be rejected". This woman will not stop her withdrawal behavior until the root issue of sadness is resolved. Once the state of sadness is effectively treated, she will experience something like a state of safety and self-acceptance, allowing her to feel good about herself. The behavior change will follow the state change, leading to more interaction with others.

Experience that is void of emotion is void of learning.

Unless a healing meta-state such as self-acceptance is brought to bear upon sadness, sadness will remain, believing itself marooned on a deserted island unaware civilization exists just over the hilltop. This state continues until sadness scales the hill observing the multitude of resources now in reach. As an analogy to states going through the meta-stating process, we might think of limiting states existing like bubbles. Each state exists rather unaware of others states and their status.

Unless calm is brought to bear upon sadness, sadness will remain, believing itself marooned on a desert island.

When we meta-state these state bubbles, they rise higher and higher, building pressure from the inside. The inevitable drive to equalize, or obtain equilibrium, wins out once the state bubble reaches a high enough meta-level. The bubble bursts, mixing its contents with the rest of the atmosphere, until it fully integrates. This describes the process and outcome of meta-stating.

If we find an especially powerful state bubble, it may contain several lower-level states under its control. Such was the case with withdrawal orchestrated by inferiority feelings orchestrated by sadness. Meta-stating this collection of states sets them all free. Maybe we feel fearful about utilizing several states as resources. If we find the state that exists meta to this fear ("How do you feel about feeling your fear?"), we may then access and remove the barrier to these states, allowing free access.

Case study
A client often experienced guilt when she thought she did not uphold others' expectations of her. This state of guilt prevented her from freely accessing other solution states. In effect, she locked herself into her guilt state. Numerous circumstances and various people could activate this guilt process in her as she let the expectations of others set her guilt in motion.

For her, this guilt state was like a big bubble. It affected many states and many situations. However, we found that the guilt state had only one trigger common to all episodes: failure to uphold others' expectations. Finding that theme allowed access to all its influences. If she could not "do" guilt she would have to respond differently to the previous triggers.

An important point here is that *an effective conscience bases itself on empathy and not guilt or shame*. To differentiate briefly, remorse and regret are about a behavior we want to change. Guilt identifies the person with the behavior and becomes self-condemning. Lifting our conscience to an empathetic level removes the former self-protective approach, making the issue more about the universal good of *all*.

Eliminating this client's ability to produce guilt meant that her higher-level values, including empathy, could guide her interaction with others.

We applied a method known as the "drop-down-through" technique developed by Tad James (Hall and Bodenhamer, 1997). This intervention applies the principles of logical levels of thought identified by Korzybski (1933, 1994). It resembles going up the meta-ladder but, instead of going up, the "drop-down-through" process goes down through states until it finds the ultimate meta-state. We can also reach our highest state by going forward or backward through states and time. Nice, knowing that any direction we move, if we go far enough, we end up at the same blissful place.

This client went to a place in which she experienced a deep sense of profound "OKness". Guilt ceased existing here. At this place there were no wrongdoings because she received guidance from her most insightful, empathetic states. Thus she experienced no need to compensate. Errors simply meant that she needed to adjust her responses. The whole problem began when she felt she had to make up for something she had done wrong. Now, unable to experience guilt, she acts in accord with her highest-level states.

These higher-level states prevent a guilt-free crime spree (in case you exception seekers were wondering!). Higher-level states rely on empathy and the common good, which runs contrary to taking advantage of others in any way. The higher-level states make her more resourceful and effective in operating herself and in relationships with others. These states naturally take others into account along with self. Higher-level states like these have the ecology, conscientiousness, built into them, or else they would not be at the highest level. Follow-up six months later revealed that she continued operating effectively without producing guilt. In this case, bursting her bubble allowed good things to happen.

This client shifted from lower-level developmental or Meta-States[R] to higher levels of human development. We move beyond guilt upon reaching the autonomous level within Loevinger's theory (1976). Not doing guilt at all may actually reflect operating from the integrated level of development. Suffice to say, she accessed higher levels and utilized them as the result of meta-stating regardless of the operating level.

Another principle about meta-states involves interpersonal conflict. Actually this may be a principle about interpersonal conflict involving meta-states. Regardless of which way it is, we find that interpersonal conflicts occur from parallel developmental-level states. Notice how I just went meta to the preceding two possible explanations. By doing this meta-move, I make the issue broader and now include both aspects instead of either/or.

If either person in a disagreement goes meta to the state utilized in the conflict, he or she approaches the issue differently, thus changing and diffusing the original conflict. Unresolved interpersonal conflicts seem to exist when the participants occupy parallel-state developmental levels. These levels can be primary states or meta-states. Einstein noted that we can't solve a problem on the level of the problem. Another way to say this is that the solution does not exist within the problem. The reason the problem exists is because it does not contain a solution in the first place.

Stepping back from a situation moves us to a meta-state providing additional and new perspectives about (meta) the problem. Only one person needs to go meta to the conflict for it to diffuse. Much as the tennis match continues only as long as each player continues hitting the ball back. If one player lays down her racket, the match ceases. This becomes the case when meta-stating one person in an interpersonal conflict. Meta-stating both people permits continuing increases in the available resources for resolving the conflict.

**One of the more wonderful characteristics of Meta-States^R
is what seems to be their natural existence—you don't
need to install them.**

Everyone possesses immediate and continuous access to these states as this ability accompanies our cerebral cortex. Asking the appropriate stimulating questions reveals the meta-state. To leave an undesirable state, simply ask yourself, "If I were not feeling this way how would I feel?" Upon eliciting this state, ask yourself,

"When I feel this state to the absolute utmost, what is this feeling?" This moves you up the meta ladder to higher Meta-States^R.

Now tune into the physical sensations associated with the most recent state. Feel this sensation wherever you may notice it within your body—your chest, stomach, wherever you may notice this sensation. Now allow the sensation to spread through your entire self until you feel it equally everywhere. Upon experiencing this, ask yourself, "What do I call this feeling?" This takes you to the next meta-level. Now feel this feeling, both emotionally and physically, to the utmost—and what do you name this state? Keep repeating this cycle until you have navigated up the winding staircase to the top for the ultimate meta-state. This staircase exists in all of us. We just seek and then we find.

There is another principle about states that helps us identify which state is associated with the emotional injury. As we have seen, symptoms of psychological disorders exist as misguided efforts to compensate for some emotional injury. But things usually don't work out so well when motivation for action comes from compensation or avoidance efforts. Sooner or later the chosen action backfires, leaving the person at the same state she was trying to leave behind. For example, the alcohol abuser uses alcohol to shift herself away from a strong sense of shame. But, after the alcohol abuse, she ends up feeling a sense of shame. The married person who has an affair to offset feelings of low self-worth ends up getting even more feelings of low self-worth.

What this compensating process tells us is that the state experienced right after the failed compensating effort is the state needing treatment. This state, be it shame, low self-worth, or any other limiting state, stems from the emotional injury. Meta-stating this limiting state can help a person move through the negative state and restore access to whatever state was abandoned at the time of the injury.

We are not our states

Our relationship with our states greatly influences whether and how we operate our states. Stepping out of any state allows the awareness that we are not our states, but we operate them. The meta-states of shame and guilt occur because we confuse self with states. I guess the primary reason why people hesitate to receive counseling is the inability to go meta to the problem state. This condition essentially makes up the problem. If you can't separate self from state, it becomes easy to experience guilt or shame by *confusing* self with state.

How can you know a person goes to a meta-position during a casual conversation? A meta-position is revealed when the conversation broadens to more general topics, including additional items or contents yet within the same category. It is a subtle process but useful to know. The client does not get off the topic or subject: she just provides additional examples. When issues broaden, progress happens. Instead of one twig, you now gain access to the whole branch.

The higher the meta-state addressed in treatment, the more effective the intervention. To identify the broader and more influential state, find the state encompassing the examples that the client describes. Do this by identifying what all the bits of information have in common. This state is the one that needs the healing. Meta-stating changes a problem state to a larger category and in turn changes the content meaning of subcategories. The principle of higher Meta-States^R ruling over lower states exemplifies itself here. We might generalize and say that the larger the frame of reference the person uses, the higher the meta-level of operating and the higher the developmental level of the person.

While primary states concern our environment, Meta-States^R concern our internal states. We may find an almost endless array of state layers consisting of meta-state upon meta-state. When this works well, the structure leads us up to our highest state of being. This state may be beyond the ability of words to describe it. However, when our structure involves an unhealed wound, the ascending stops at the point of the wound. The block remains unless we associate into the wounded state and then carry its awareness up to new heights. By remaining unconscious of it, we allow the wounded state to reign. The layers of Meta-States^R vary from person to person. We might find that each layer gets "born" into awareness, or recruited, resulting from life experiences. The more layers present, the more need for intervening states. Adverse experiences seem especially likely to prompt additional states into the mix.

This state layering effect requires a sifting or sorting when we intervene. Restoring the free use of a resourceful meta-state requires we move back through meta-time, arriving at the state in its original status. This state feels the wound. This state of origin recruited the other meta-states as protecting devices, so these recruited states correspond to a time of injury or re-injury. We may operate from a state of anger for protecting our state of vulnerability. We may then move to a state that exists meta to the original primary state and first meta-state.

If anger works for protecting at that moment, then we keep the structure. If it proves ineffective we move to a state above it, adding, we hope, a more effective meta-state. Placing protective states between our self and the environment seems to be human nature. We perform this act rather than recruit resources from on high. Again, though, this buffering response stems from attributing power over our states to external forces. It seems our first response to conflict, unless otherwise tempered, is to recruit primary states with narrow awareness to fight against the supposed environmental enemy. But, in truth, we are always our only enemy.

The next portion deals with how we can reclaim "lost", forgotten, or injured states from our "past". How do we track back in meta-time and inject the original state with the needed antidote? We'll now look at the process.

Crossing state lines

This method of restoring equilibrium addresses the symptom structure as basing itself on a series of compensatory Meta-States[R]. Abandoning the midrange states brings in two or three compensating states to superimpose upon the original one. These states also contain certain shifts from equilibrium in thought, emotions, and behaviors. The initial error involves departing from midrange states. We will use the example of the person who does not trust others after a series of relationships in which she trusted too much. Now she claims she just can't trust anyone anymore. This displays the common process of one extreme that does not work satisfactorily, followed by another extreme that also frustrates successful resolution.

A person utilizes the extreme version of a state because she believes the middle state or state of equilibrium to be off-limits. The person mistrusting others also mistrusts her own trusting ability. However, holding this strategy in place requires that she also trust her mistrusting of trusting. Tracing from the outermost state of trusting back across state lines, we then cross into the state of mistrusting. We backtrack until the original state evidences itself, trust of self in this case. It will always show itself because it initiates the whole process and will thereby be present in the whole person. The "problem", if one exists, involves shifting the state location from internal to external. We move self-trust (internal) to others-trust (external).

The next step toward restoring equilibrium involves returning the limiting state back to the way it once functioned–trust of self. Trusting ability exists, but, for the problem structure, it just shifted backward in its orientation. It relied on trusting others instead of self. Because of this, it did not work effectively. Remembering the state of trust in general permits the next step.

Solidifying the feeling associated with the trusting process then allows access to trust of trust. This remembering may include identifying the traits of self-trust, maybe that "gut feeling" that never fails us. Once we identify the benefit of self-trust, we can then notice that the only "failure" was when we did not trust our self. This reclaimed configuration of self-trust is then applied to what had been problems. The person rethinks the issues and forms new beliefs and responses while occupying the state of equilibrium or trust for this situation.

The person who can't feel good about feeling good about herself is another example of crossing state lines to restore equilibrium. She believes she must feel bad about feeling good about herself.

However, using the crossing-state-lines process, we find this person actually feels good about feeling bad about feeling good. Now we come across the point of origin or state of equilibrium. Some event in her life made it not permissible to feel good about herself directly. Yet she creatively finds ways to feel good. Once the person has associated back into the original state of "feeling good", she can experience this state.

Now, from the state of equilibrium, feeling good about self, she rethinks and forms new beliefs about feeling bad to feel good. Previously, the constricted perception in childhood ruled the process. She went through an adjustment process to find and associate into just the right amount of feeling good about self. She knew too little or too much would not work best.

The first step for crossing state lines is associating the client into the limiting state.

The first step in crossing state lines is associating the client into the limiting state. Include components of both the emotional and physical sensations. Elicit his term for describing how he feels when in this limiting state. Use questions such as, "How do you feel when you want to express yourself but believe you can't?" Follow this with something like, "Where do you feel this emotion physically? Perhaps you sense it in some part of you body." Getting details about the emotion and physical sensations helps the person associate more fully into the state. This makes for a more thorough change.

Once the client is well aware of the limiting state, simply ask, "If you did not feel [the limiting desired state], what would you be feeling?" This triggers awareness of the state that recruited protection in the first place-the original state. It picked up the shield. In this case the shield comes in the form of a negative (disengaging) state. There is no need to deal with the surface-layer negative state beyond using it as a stepping stone. Once the original positive resource state is strengthened, it willfully releases it shield.

Associating into the original positive state makes up the second step. It supposedly once lacked sufficient strength to deal with some SEE, so it seemed to need protecting. The original resource state likely feels lacking in the present day as well, in spite of the fact that the SEE was a past event. It still perceives reality from its age at the time of the SEE. This perception includes some or all of the Piagetian cognitive styles.

The original resource state that experienced a SEE continues perceiving from whatever limitations of perception were present at the time of the SEE.

Once you have associated the client into the original state, proceed to meta-state this state. When you reach one or two states above the original, be sure to include the kinesthetic in the process. This means inquiring about the kinesthetic shifts the person notes from the initial negative state he first experienced. What does he now notice? Does he have a different sensation than before, and where does it lodge? Upon eliciting this, get full details about the components of the kinesthetic.

Now determine whether the kinesthetic centers in just an isolated area, such as the upper chest or gut. Invite the client to allow the pleasant sensations to flow throughout his being, making sure the kinesthetic spreads fully. Now proceed with the linguistic meta-stating again, combining this with the kinesthetic meta-stating just described. Continue this until the person reaches his ultimate meta-state with corresponding ultimate kinesthetic meta-state.

The final step involves re-examining the old situation from the restored state for a more resourceful perspective and response choice. Also include new belief-forming. Do this by asking, "What beliefs about yourself do you now get to release?" and "What do you now believe about yourself instead?" Future-pace the new belief after applying the new resources to the issue of concern.

Once we reach the wounded state and inject it with the awareness boost brought by Meta-States[R], the healing begins. The next step involves future-pacing. This allows the person a glimpse and experience of his future through his imaginings. If you doubt the power of what you imagine to evoke thoughts, emotions, and behaviors, just consider the influence of fear. It revolves around what may happen, but has not yet happened, yet we react as if it were happening. Future-pacing generates a sort of meta-future.

We can then bring this future into our present, aligning our current behavior with our desired future. The following section provides an example of utilizing our future for shaping our present.

If you doubt the power of what you imagine to evoke thought, emotions and behavior just consider the influence of fear.

Meta-motivation: making your future your present, now

Motivation qualifies as a precious commodity. It remains in great demand and is highly valued. Demand seems constantly to out-strip supply. Those who freely access their motivation usually control their own destiny more effectively. The motivation to which I refer in this section involves the kind people use when pursuing life-enhancing goals. These goals result in positive change without adverse consequences. We could describe them as "meta-motivation". It involves defining, pursuing and achieving higher-level goals.

Time may be the most common thief of motivation—specifically the time span between action and achievement. The longer the time span, the more challenging to sustain motivation. Recommendations for maintaining motivation often point to breaking down the ultimate goal into segments. This may allow some sense of achievement at regular intervals. This segmenting of a task will supposedly add up to the final goal over time. However, even this strategy leaves gaps in time without reinforcement. During these gaps, we must essentially use our imagination to remind ourselves of the eventual reward, usually a feeling, we anticipate experiencing upon completion of the segment.

Time may be the most common thief of motivation. Specifically the time span between action and achievement.

Even this strategy is derailed when the person looks too far ahead and sees the segment dwarfing in comparison to the still distant final goal. So how do we find and maintain motivation?

Imagine a person who wants to lose 10 pounds (4.5 kilograms) to fulfill a New Year resolution. Going meta to the singular goal, we can find a more powerful motivation. What is losing 10 pounds a part of in this person's life? It may be that the meta level to losing 10 pounds is wellness for this person. This goal includes a more complete lifestyle change, not just losing 10 pounds. By expanding the goal to a larger frame, we include additional thoughts, feelings, and behaviors, creating a larger shift in lifestyle consistent with wellness. We then go meta to this and continue climbing the meta ladder until we reach the top rung. The series of Meta-States^R may go something like this: security as meta to wellness, with peace, then unity, with their higher power following. Now the person can ring in the New Year with wellness or her ultimate goal, and unity with her higher power, as the New Year resolution.

> **By encompassing additional thoughts, emotions, and behaviors, we create a larger shift in lifestyle consistent with wellness.**

Now associate the person into whatever meta-level she chooses above the original goal. Several significant results occur:

1. Instant and continuous availability of the desired state now exists. Wait no more. The emotional state experience exists here and now. The state naturally self-reinforces or supplies its own motivation. Ask the person to look out into the future and notice how living a lifestyle of wellness or unity automatically causes her to generate and sustain the goal once she has achieved it.

2. For boosting the compelling power of the meta-motivation, ask her to see the future as living in the meta-state for weeks and even months continuously. How does this feel? This creates another meta-state in and of itself consistent with and strengthening for the first meta-state. A gestalt forms by collecting the accumulating future experiences and bundling them into one powerful state. Then ask the person to reach out into the future and pull her future into herself now. "Make your future your present, now. How does this feel?" Associate her into this state fully. Future-pace again for this state.

3. Do a reversal of cause-and-effect with this method. Rather than lose 10 pounds to gain wellness or other meta-state, the state of wellness or unity will naturally self-organize, causing healthy weight. Wellness or unity causes weight loss rather than weight loss hopefully leading to wellness or unity.
4. The person would have to leave the state to lose. Since the smaller behaviors hold as their purpose generating the meta-state, the person would essentially leave the state only for the purpose of eventually experiencing the state. Why would they ever leave?

Moral: you can lose your wait to lose your weight.

The example just described demonstrates how the principles of meta-motivation apply to life processes. The real merit of the concept resides in how broadly it applies in life. For any specific goal simply find the meta-state to it for more power. This makes a compelling lifestyle.

Imagine a person who wants to become a nonsmoker. Upon accomplishing this goal what does she believe she would experience? Access this state and associate her into it. Chunk up for maximum power. Now encourage her to find alternatives for the undesired behavior that is ecologically sound. Do this from her ultimate meta-state, such as unity with her higher power. By-products will naturally be consistent with this state. Now, future-pace the alternative lifestyle. Turbo-charge this with the future extension. Ask the client to see herself many weeks, and months in a row choosing thoughts, emotions, and behaviors from her ultimate meta-state. Identify the state of living and sustaining the meta-state. At this point ask her to reach out into her future and pull it into herself now. "Make your future your present, now." Fully associate her into this state. Future-pace again. Now she is ready to go and manifest her state of state manifesting.

Ask the client to see herself many days, weeks, and months in a row choosing thought, emotions and behaviors from her ultimate meta-state.

Consider the person who wants to write an article for a journal. First, find and access the meta-state above the immediate goal and then move up to the ultimate meta-state. Associate him into this state. As a sidelight, wasn't he already in a meta-state when he came up with the idea of writing the article? Anyway, now he is associated into a meta-state well above the one that was meta to the stuck spot. So actually the only way he cannot write the article is to leave the state he desires and occupies now.

The general process consists of laying the "meta-train" track in such a configuration that the short-term goal becomes tied to the track. In the course of following the "meta-railway" the person propels self to and through the immediate goal. The ultimate result becomes destination unlimited.

How do we switch meta-tracks to one that allows free use of our deepest resources? Perhaps without parallel, the most significant factor in creating change is detecting differences in our environment. By doing so we break the trance we lived in, permitting us freedom of choice for our responses. Trances sustain themselves on detecting similarities. Perceiving differences provides the opportunity for dealing with the environment in a new, more aware, way that is fully in the present instead of how it resembles the past.

The difference is the difference

Two particular points will serve as illustration. The first is that meta-programs function as support and defense systems to the states Hall (1995, 2000) identifies as Meta-States^R. Meta-programs are not arbitrary or coincidental styles of processing the world and its stimuli. Rather, they result from unconscious choices permitting feelings of safety and perpetuating the organism. Ideally, we can select or shift meta-programs as best suits any given situation. Choosing the best version of a meta-program occurs in accordance with protecting or maintaining the meta-state.

Experiences seem to be initially sorted by the mind as a threat to, an aid to, or neutral toward our states' continued existence.

We call neutral stimuli boring. The other two categories either threaten the existence of a state or assist the state to survive. This three-branch decision-tree process apparently represents separate meta-programs operating meta to the other programs.

At unconscious levels, decision-making takes place about how to filter the information in the environment. This decision predicates itself on keeping the primary or meta-state "alive". We tend to perceive in ways that perpetuate the Meta-States^R we occupy. What lets us change filtering programs or prevents us from changing our filtering programs? The programs serve to preserve or prevent states-they each represent toward or away from strategies. They act as rudders steering us toward or away from states in an ocean full of states. Changing programs may maintain a meta-state we desire and not changing may prevent a state, meta or otherwise, that we believe threatens us. Additionally, we can actually change Meta-States^R by shifting meta-programs. Two examples follow, one fictional and general, the other one factual and specific.

The first example of relations between meta-programs and meta-states involves a movie from 1995 titled *The Englishman Who Went Up a Hill but Came Down a Mountain*. I thought the movie was quite good and the scenery even better. Set in the lovely countryside of Wales, this movie revolves around the residents of a small Welsh town who want a particular piece of land to be officially declared a "mountain". If it is declared an official mountain, the area and the environs around it will be considered the gateway to Wales and the mountainous region of the UK. If, however, the height of the land is just a hill, then the people will feel they are insignificant. The residents spend the time in the film going to great lengths to insure that the official British survey team, led by "the Englishman", finds that the mountain is tall enough to qualify. At first the surveyors find the height of the hill insufficient to qualify as a mountain.

From this point on, the townspeople come up with countless methods to delay the survey team from leaving the little town. The literal last-ditch effort involves moving dirt from the land below to the top of the hill while delaying the surveyors. A reassessment is then agreed and the hill now becomes a mountain, saving the worth of the area for the residents. Here's the parallel to meta-programs. All of the efforts by the locals are similar to meta programs: their efforts were all designed to preserve the valuable meta-state or feelings of worth in this case. People go to great lengths and distortions to maintain a meta-state.

This next case serves as an example of changing meta-programs and, in so doing, changing Meta-States^R. For anxiety disorders to sustain themselves, it seems, people must sort their environment by way of similarities rather than differences. This may also be true for most, if not all, maladaptive behaviors. To some extent people may also sort by global perspective alone rather than detail as well. The similarities relate back to the original SEE for such people.

People with a trauma in the past actually believe that in order to feel safe they must look at each situation to find how the current resembles the original SEE. They seem to believe that by identifying potential dangers they can stay safe. However, sorting by this process ends up maintaining the already limiting state. The person wants to feel calm but he cannot find any reasons to do so. These people are just looking at the wrong stimuli. As a result they find reasons to feel anxious in any circumstance remotely similar to the first anxiety-provoking event. After enough overgeneralizing, just about every situation bears some resemblance to he original traumatic event.

By changing what a person looks for in the environment to sorting for differences, she could find reasons to believe she is safe. We could say that sorting for similarities acts as a major influence in maintaining anxiety disorders, for the majority of limiting states. How else do we perpetuate them?

We could say that sorting for similarities rather than differences acts as a major influence in maintaining anxiety disorders, for the majority of limiting states.

Case study
The client in this example is a well-educated woman in her fifties who holds a graduate degree. Margaret spends a sizable portion

of her work presenting to and facilitating groups in her role as a management and business consultant. She comes to the counseling session with me and says she wants relief from her anxiety. She reports a "fear of people". Essentially, she has a social phobia.

Using her good insight, she had already traced the root of her social discomfort to a time in the sixth grade. She just didn't know how to relieve it; instead she just relived it. She transferred to a different school during the sixth grade. This new school apparently had many delinquents in it. The memory she used as representing the utmost in anxiety was an incident in the girls' restroom. Other girls in the restroom were throwing toilet-paper rolls over the walls of the restroom stall that she was in and they were verbally harassing her. While this one incident stood out to her, the entire school year was filled with confrontations with a rowdy bunch of students.

In the next school year she began junior high. This was a much better experience and she was around a lot of students who were very different from those of the previous year. In spite of a calm atmosphere, from that point forward she kept experiencing fear of other people. She described nervousness and feelings of impending doom and believed that others were negatively judging her. This collection of beliefs, associated emotions, and behaviors greatly impaired Margaret's ability to do her job effectively.

Once we made sure of the issue that Margaret wanted help with, ridding herself of social anxiety, we then identified how she perceives her current environment. The first thing I wanted to know was, when she presented information in public, what did she observe around her and what did it mean? Margaret described feeling threatened just by the presence of other people in the room. She expected them to find fault with her and expected herself to behave perfectly. If the audience had questions, she experienced more distress, even if the questions were reasonable and she knew the answer. She attributed great power to others and believed they had little tolerance of her. Margaret based much of this belief on how the audience was dressed—business suits for both males and females.

At this point it became apparent that considerable differences existed between the people who were present when Margaret developed her anxiety and the people she now knew. I asked her to notice the ways the two groups were different. At first she had trouble doing this because she had been so used to sorting the situations by similarities. I assisted her by pointing out how those unruly students in the past could not now be these executives now. If they were, they would have had to change their ways somewhere along the line, perhaps by early in high school. The students would have had to change the delinquent style even further in order to finish college, and now hold responsible positions in their company.

Her face began showing shifts in emotions as the emotional strain left. She then began to notice other differences between the past and now. By this time, separate categories existed for the people in the present and the people of the past. She felt relief and calm. Creating separate mental categories for past and present information was an essential step in relieving past trauma. Sorting for differences helped this new category come into being.

> **Creating separate mental categories for past and present information was an essential step in relieving past trauma.**

The next step involved driving a permanent wedge between the old and new perceptions. This would prevent the future merging of the two distinctly different categories. I asked her to allow her mind to come up with something that would remind her of the difference between the past and now. She soon began to laugh. You know, we can literally laugh off limiting states. She told me that the image she chose that would remind her of the difference was of a man in a suit standing up over the restroom stall wall getting ready to throw over a roll of toilet paper. I don't know about you, but when I picture a man in a suit with a roll of toilet paper in his hand ready to throw it, I start smiling.

Margaret now clearly knew that her old fear was ridiculous. It was completely incompatible with reality in the present day. After having some fun with this image and the associated emotions, we future-paced the new states and finished with an ecology check. She was ready to go without fear. Follow-up in three months revealed continued calm and resourceful ways of being. What makes the difference? *The difference between the past and the present is the difference.*

Let's look a little further at the role that sorting for differences or similarities plays in our daily functioning. We live out most of our in a trance state. We look for the usual stimuli and launch into the usual response set with little thought given to our response. Whether we sort for similarities or differences determines whether our trance remains intact or breaks. Sorting for similarities creates a bridge or chain of similar material, basing itself on common factors. We just move along step after usual step. Once we begin seeking and sorting for differences, we awake from our trance, thereby freeing ourselves of the pattern of thoughts, emotions, and behaviors associated with the similar. We create new awareness, thus arriving at choice.

The case study represents only one example of how meta-programs play a role in sustaining Meta-States^R. This particular one allows separating old learning from new learning. Once this separation is completed, then new learning and resources can take over the operating function. By shifting meta-programs we can influence and shift Meta-States^R.

Two general styles exist for experiencing life: analyzing and experiencing. Some theories call the analyzing style a "through-time orientation". The experiencing style is known as an "in-time orientation". Consider the person who organizes his timeline in a through-time manner—the analyzer. This person may limit himself and his experience of life and emotions. Changing from through-time to in-time, the experiencer, would likely result in different Meta-States^R, which could provide solutions to former limitations. It would at least increase the resourcefulness of this person. He could then choose the time orientation better suited to each situation. What Meta-States^R might that open up for him?

Consider how choice applies to all the meta-programs.

Accessing and installing the versatility to operate from any perceptual style can permit reaching higher Meta-States^R when we seem stymied. In fact, when meta-stating someone and then having them re-examine a situation, haven't they also shifted meta-programs? Which permits which? Cognitive therapy (Beck, 1976) is all about changing filters or meta-programs in order to change Meta-States[R], thereby permitting more resourceful positions of operating oneself. Through either route of change, symbolically, you end up with a ship that has a rudder allowing left and right turns instead of predicating all maneuvers on the limiting ability of left turns only.

We might think of any injured part as experiencing distress and seeking healing in its own limited way. The part tries over and over for relief but usually through the same method—first-order change. The same method applied to the same problem yields the same outcome. If the problem remains the same, only new methods yield new outcomes. Therapy holds this as its purpose. But how do we access the part needing treatment? All too often the last straw gets the most attention when the catalyst remains undiscovered. Look back to the syndrome of the workaholic who feels discomfort with contentment and doubts about her competence.

Sometimes a person coming in for therapy only presents a series of unsuccessful attempts at feeling better. He just describes various methods of achieving frustration. The person who experiences doubts about his competence continually attempts to verify competence. It seems as though his "convincer" strategy for this competence can't be satisfied and remains on a "continual" mode.

A "convincer strategy" refers to the number of times a person needs to see, hear, or feel something to become convinced it is so. Each person has this strategy and applies it to experiences throughout life. How many times do you need to see, hear, or feel someone do something to be convinced they are competent? Usually, the answer ranges from two to four. However, some people need experience only one example of competence before feeling convinced. Other people may exhibit a strategy known as "continual".

People using a "continual-convincer strategy" approach each example as if no history preceded it. No matter what you say or do, they never become believers. Nothing or no one but themselves will convince them. While we possess one convincer strategy about other people, we may use another strategy for ourselves. This different convincer strategy may account for a person who is harder on herself than on others. In particular I believe we employ a continual convincer strategy within unconscious parts. Why else would an achieving person never feel she accomplishes enough? Such a person never becomes convinced that she possesses competence.

I suspect we apply this continual convincer strategy to every state we fear. It never seems to feel safe to experience a state known as calm or a state known as competence, assertiveness, trust, or some state of equilibrium. This exists as a built-in safety mechanism. Some people fear that if they become convinced of their competence, for example, they would then experience what they fear even more. The strategy's design aims at stopping short of the state most feared. The motto here is, "You can't let your guard down so never become convinced." There is always just one more hurdle to jump for access to the state. This remains unfinished, just as tomorrow never comes. It feels safer this way.

Some people fear that if they become convinced of their competence, for example, they would then experience a state they fear even more.

Intervening in the case of the continual convincer strategy involves finding what state would occur if the person actually became convinced he was competent or experienced some other fended-off state. The natural temptation for the therapist concerns stepping in the quicksand by participating in the method that says, "Fill up the belief-discrepancy gap with examples." The therapist joins the client at the client's level of behavior, which generates frustration by finding and identifying examples of competence.

Soon, the client feels incompetent for frustrating the therapist and the therapist feels tempted to find another label for this "purposeful" frustrating client who "resists" the therapist's efforts. If the therapist remains on the level of the client, both experience frustration. The effective therapist steps into a position that is meta to the client's situation.

Until we perceive from a higher meta-state, we can't extract ourselves from the limiting loop of the continual convincer strategy. In this case, the therapist may ask the client what he will feel upon becoming convinced of his competence. This again draws the person into a state that is meta to the one at which he is stuck. Imagine experiencing the desired result and consequent mental state. Meta-state this state and then re-examine and reconfigure the original "problem" utilizing the new state and increase in associated awareness. For the continual convincer applied to competence, find the state that happens after he has been convinced of competence. This accesses the driving state. It may seem the person fears the state of competence, but the fear often occupies the place just one level above where the fighting happens. The emotional fight within the person is not really about competence, competence is just the battleground.

When the competence issue settles, the real issue surfaces. Maybe the client states, upon being convinced of competence, he would experience a state of "contentment". This state likely endures the injury. Now build on this state, meta-stating "contentment" above and beyond to freedom or peace, for example. Add the usual elements of reviewing the formerly troubling situation. Future-pace by extending the meta-state out over a period of days, weeks, and months. Now form a gestalt of this state by asking, "How does it feel to you when you effectively experience this state [freedom or peace in this example] for days, weeks, months, and years into the future?" This process activates the state more deeply in the client. The client forms new beliefs about self as the old fall away. Then just future-pace this new belief. Yes, future-pace the future-pacing to layer the Meta-States^R into a gestalt of effectiveness.

Regardless of the diagnosis or dysfunction, it seems this process of the "continual convincer" comes into play. A behavioral loop intends to get relief but finds only frustration. This happens because the looping behavior works at a level parallel to the problem. It knows strategies only for feeling competent and the person must avoid this state because it leads to the dreaded state of contentment. It tries and tries with all its limited ability. Effective results come from operating at levels above the problem.

Continual accomplishing will never convince the person that feeling competent is safe because of the consequences initially encountered after feelings of competence-punishment in some form for experiencing contentment. Experiencing and operating from "freedom" or "peace" permits additional choices and resources. When competence ascends to states such as freedom or peace, the loop ceases. This process again demonstrates the principles of "if some is good, more is better" and "people change always and only for higher meta-levels".

Chapter Twelve
Piaget Revisited

Keeping in mind our previous discussion about states of equilibrium and disequilibrium and the techniques for altering and restoring the former, I will finish with the cognitive characteristics of a person who utilizes states of equilibrium. Piaget (1965) originally identified the following traits as common to states of equilibrium. He referred to the first quality of equilibrium as the "field of application".

Characteristics of equilibrium

1. Field of application

By "field of application", Piaget meant the size of the chunk perceived at any given time. In childhood, we perceive in a very limited field of application, owing to our centering. However, by early puberty we possess the ability to expand our awareness. Through this increased awareness we gain access to more information, thereby increasing perceptual accuracy. The "bigger picture" becomes available to us. Because of broader awareness, we can account for, assess, and respond to more factors on a broader scale, permitting more effective choices in life. Field of application may be thought of as our field of awareness. This field, regardless of size, determines what material we have available for assimilating and accommodating.

I tend to refer to this field-of-application concept as continuum thinking. In other words, rather than consider one point on a continuum, consider the whole spectrum along the continuum from one end to the other. Continuum thinking is the opposite of centering. Very often, a client comes in for therapy, in part due to being at the affect of his centering. By being helped to gain awareness of the whole continuum of an issue, a client can consider many other resources and response options. Sometimes, I intentionally suggest extreme response options at each end of the continuum. This can, of course, be done with good humor. What happens for the client after he has loosened both his mood and perceptions is that he then gains flexibility of thought, emotion, and behavior.

Taking more information into consideration permits more sensitive and effective responses. We do not respond to a single word or sentence from someone. Rather we consider the preceding sentences, behavior, larger context, and possible future implications. We possess and utilize the ability to go to a meta-level to observe the whole situation. As we saw earlier, we can generally determine the developmental level of a person by the size of his or her frame of reference. Another way of changing states by changing meta-programs is through expanding the field of awareness. With a larger field of application a person works with broader and larger categories of information and thought. By using this skill we more effectively achieve and maintain equilibrium.

2. Mobility

Mobility is another characteristic of equilibrium. This trait exists in a sort of meta-position to the field of application. Where the previous trait involved expanded awareness, mobility refers to the capacity for moving one's field of application between clusters of information. This allows comparisons of multiple fields, offsetting the early-childhood perception style of either/or. We create this mobility when we compare limiting beliefs and their foundation to both beliefs that provide us with freedom and the infinite roots of these freeing beliefs. Mobility is how we know some is good and more is better, by comparing chunks. Positive resource states possess deeper, wiser, and more extensive roots. This is how resource states win out as our choice if we let ourselves access them.

Mobility is another trait of equilibrium. Mobility is the capacity to move one's field of application between clusters of information, allowing comparison.

3. Permanence

Permanence represents another trait of equilibrium. This concept involves the enduring nature of the equilibrium. Regardless of the nature of the input, the system consistently maintains equilibrium. Imagine a person who experiences an unwanted outcome at a time when he was in a state of joy. He does not reject the state of joy but rather remains aware of and embraces the benefits of joy as a state independent of circumstances. Permanence overcomes such cognitive deficits as transductive logic, where the state at the time of adversity was blamed for the problem and rejected because of the unwanted outcome. By exhibiting permanence, a person can sustain resourceful states or freely access them again in the future.

Stability is the most important trait of equilibrium. This refers to the ability to compensate for unsteadying influences. No matter how you tilt the bowl of water, the water always finds its level.

4. Stability

Stability is the final and most important quality of equilibrium. Stability refers to the ability to compensate or essentially cancel out unsteadying influences. Some refer to this trait as reversibility. This reversibility develops after the child outgrows her irreversibility style of thinking. Reversibility allows a person to offset temporary displacement from equilibrium to return to equilibrium. Imagine a bowl half full of water. No matter how you tilt the bowl of water, the water always finds its level. In life, once we assimilate information, if we find our current state or response does not work, we accommodate. Accommodating means shifting states or responses to one more suitable for the situation. The result is stable equilibrium. This greatly resembles permanence. Some within the field of developmental psychology find no difference.

Stability means we possess consistent ability for shifting states at will, finding the one that permits our desired outcome. No matter the obstacle or change in the environment, we find, access, and occupy the state fitting the task. After we utilize a state, stability means that we naturally and easily return to equilibrium. This ability to return to the balanced center offsets the childhood cognitive trait of irreversibility. One simple yet practical definition of mental health may be the ability to shift states constructively at will. This can occur consciously or unconsciously.

These four traits—field of application, mobility, permanence, and stability—combine to provide enough cognitive power for overcoming the former cognitive limitations of childhood. Notice how all effective counseling promotes these qualities. Notice how effective people apply and exhibit these qualities. Through any and all effective counseling, people elevate themselves, their states, and system as a whole. This elevating process involves one form or another of meta-stating, which raises and expands our awareness, allowing us to reclaim our original balanced whole self.

I will add a few more traits of equilibrium to the four described above:

5. Foresight

Foresight refers to the ability of a person to look ahead and imagine consequences of potential behavior. He can anticipate outcomes and thus consider more information before actually deciding on a course of events. Foresight is essentially the opposite of impulsiveness. States of equilibrium possess foresight, allowing thoughtful choices rather than spur-of-the-moment reactive behavior. You can also relate the concept and process of foresight to Piaget's concept of centering. Centering lacks foresight skills while foresight results in dilated awareness, decentering.

6. Patience

Patience plays a crucial role in states of equilibrium. Without patience we tend to behave impulsively and without foresight. Patience allows us to wait for more information to come into our awareness, thus making a more informed decision about any given situation. Patience is not passivity. Patience is the result of realizing that, if we pause briefly before deciding, we may gain better perspective about a situation and override our initial emotional, impulse-driven response. We can take more information into account, enabling us to make a better-tailored response.

7. Flexibility

Flexibility represents the last of the triumvirate, foresight and patience being the other two. Flexibility allows us to adjust our response to any given situation. Flexibility allows us to choose our response based on the desired outcome rather than some ego-driven choice that often backfires. Flexibility means that we have access to any and all of our states so we can draw from the full array, increasing our effectiveness. Flexibility also means we can look at a situation in many ways, not just the first one that comes to mind. Here, flexibility means versatility of thought, emotion, and behavior. Take a 360-degree look at any situation to get the best view, receive the most information, and ultimately make the best response choice. But to acquire this 360-degree perspective we rely on foresight, patience, and flexibility. When I think about the vast majority of issues, or "problems", that clients bring into the counseling session, each usually lacks these three ingredients of foresight, patience and flexibility.

8. Personalizing

Personalizing, or rather, *not* personalizing, any event that happens is another powerfully influential feature of states of equilibrium. When we personalize another person's behavior or any event that happens in our life, two particular dysfunctional thought processes occur. First, personalizing another's thoughts, emotions, or behavior means we believe we caused the event (transductive logic) and thus must take responsibility for it and perhaps fix the other's status if it is problematic. The other things that happen when we personalize is that we then become in danger of drawing conclusions about ourselves (inductive logic) as a result of "causing" the other person's thoughts, emotion, or behavior. Once we have personalized (in other words, taken responsibility for the other and formed a limiting belief about ourselves), we then take steps to fix a situation, based on an illusion to begin with!

Accurate perception of self and others restores equilibrium. In the case of not personalizing, we recognize another person's thoughts, emotions, or behavior as being strictly a product of that person's inner world and his maps of the world. Once we separate ourselves from the other person we can empathize yet remain an intact, separate entity. Not personalizing also stops the detrimental effects of drawing conclusions about ourselves. Once we separate our whole self from any event, we recognize that our whole self continuously exists as a whole, regardless of which single state or cluster of states we may use.

In another, slight variation, not personalizing means not jumping to conclusions or generalizations about the value of ourselves. While we make mistakes in our thinking, emotional states, and behaviors, these do not represent our whole self, just a portion that may be misapplied. These errors do not change our whole self, thus no conclusion about self, other than being a whole being, can ever accurately apply. By not personalizing we permanently suspend judgment of ourselves.

9. Locus of control

Locus of control makes up another crucial feature of states of equilibrium. As we have seen, an external locus of control means that the person possessing it believes that external events control her destiny. The person with an *internal* locus of control believes that she, as an individual, determines her own destiny. Events out of her control may happen, but her reaction is fully self-contained and self-determined. She steers her own ship and decides the course she will take.

The significance of possessing an internal locus of control in gaining equilibrium comes from knowing where your states of mind reside and who chooses which states to utilize. Also, the internal-locus person does not perceive external events as threatening the existence of any states, allowing any and all states to remain at her disposal. By possessing an internal locus of control, the individual becomes immune to the thinking flaws that Piaget identified as characterizing childhood. This immunity allows unencumbered state choice and resting equilibrium.

10. Trust

Trust makes up another feature of states of equilibrium. Here, trust means that the person trusts himself, allowing free communication within. This free communication within permits him to access any state and to trust that the state is a positive resource. Trusting himself, he can know what he wants and needs, which allows use of this awareness. He will trust the clarity of that awareness. Trust permits a full, unadulterated use of any state, while doubt dilutes the purity and strength of a state. You know how you behave when you doubt yourself or your state: you hold back. But when you fully trust yourself and your state you utilize them with great gusto, creating more influence in situations and a better outcome.

11. Continuum of thinking

Continuum of thinking represents another core characteristic of states of equilibrium. I use this term because it means that we recognize that, with any single perspective, it simply represents a given point along a continuum. We can identify a continuum of responses from one extreme to the other. By first stretching out awareness to each extreme, we free our thinking to choose any point between the extreme of possible points. One of the ways we limit our responses is by limiting our thinking. If we first assess any given situation by noticing what is happening at the extreme responses, we remove the constricting thoughts and awareness, promoting the use of foresight, flexibility, and patience.

12. Mistaken causality

A final trait common to states of equilibrium, or one that promotes states of equilibrium, is the concept that there is no such thing as cause (no transductive logic allowed!). An excellent book by Dennis and Jennifer Chong (1991) nicely describes the pitfalls of believing in and searching for causes of events. As I mentioned earlier, cause does not exist, just correlation. You would have to start at the beginning of time to identify all the variables that *influenced*, not caused any outcome. This amounts to the concept that everything influences everything, so what will you do now? There is no blame, only choice and solutions.

Now we come to the end of this theoretical exploration for the time being. And you may wonder what gave rise to this book and the equilibrium theory. These ideas came to me after I had worked for many years with many clients. The spine for this body of work comes from the concepts developed by Michael Hall. His descriptions of states, meta-states, and their dynamics led me to realize the influence of states in our personality. In the course of therapy, the client and I would find that treatment was complete when states of equilibrium were reclaimed. It became apparent to me that, while I may work with many client issues, the overriding issue, meta to the specific client issue, was restoring equilibrium. Clients would consistently declare that they finished therapy feeling complete, comfortable, and whole, after quenching their need for equilibrium. I decided to explore the "problem-making" process and the solution-making process more deeply. I benefited from and relied on many theories that I used as lenses through which to view client dynamics. As a result of this search, I came to believe that the driving force and fabric weaving this whole helix of personal evolution is this drive for equilibrium. Through this book I have tried to present the complex interplay between concepts that forms the dynamics of the equilibrium–disequilibrium play. I hope you found this interesting, thought-provoking, and helpful.

Bibliography

American Psychiatric Association, 1994, *Diagnostic and Statistical Manual of Mental Disorders*, 4th ed., Washington, DC.

Andreas, Connirae & Andreas, Tamara, 1994, *Core Transformations: Reaching the Wellspring Within*, Real People Press, Moab, UT.

Andreas, Steve & Andreas, Connirae, 1989, *Heart of the Mind*, Real People Press, Moab, UT.

Bandura, Albert, 1977, *Social Learning Theory*, Prentice-Hall, Englewood Cliffs, NJ.

Bandler, Richard & Grinder, John, 1975, *The Structure of Magic*, Science and Behavioral Books, Palo Alto, CA.

Bateson, Gregory, 1972, *Steps to an Ecology of Mind*, Balentine, New York.

Beck, Aaron, 1976, *Cognitive Therapy and the Emotional Disorders*, International University Press, New York.

Benson, H. & Klepper, M. Z., 1976, *The Relaxation Response*, Avon Books, New York.

Burns, David, 1980, *Feeling Good: The New Mood Therapy*, New American Library, New York.

Cannon, Walter, 1932, *The Wisdom of the Body*, Norton, New York.

Chong, Dennis & Jennifer, 1991, *Don't Ask Why: A book About the Structure of Blame, Bad Communications and Miscommunications*, C-Jade Publishing , Inc., Oakville, Ontario.

Clifford, G. J., 1984, *Edward Thorndike: The Sane Positivist*, Wesleyan University Press, Middleton, PA.

Cofer, C. N. & Apply, M. H., 1964, *Motivation: Theory and Research*, Wiley, New York.

D'Andrea, Michael, 1984, *The Counselor as Pacer: A Model for Revitalization of the Counseling Profession*, Counseling and Human Development (February).

Dilts, Robert & McDonald, Roberts, 1995, *Tools of the Spirit*, Meta Publications, Carpolita, CA.

Donaldson, Margaret, 1979, *Children's Minds*, W. W. Norton, New York.

Elkind, David, 1994, *Understanding Your Child from Birth to Sixteen*, Allyn & Bacon, Boston.

Erikson, Erik, 1963, *Childhood and Society*, W. W. Norton, New York.

Festinger, Leon, 1957, *A Theory of Cognitive Dissonance*, Harper and Row, New York.

Flavell, John, 1963, *The Developmental Psychology of Jean Piaget*, Van Nordstrand, Princeton, NJ.

Freud, Sigmund, 1914, *Psychopathology of Everyday Life*, Macmillan, New York.

Hall, Michael, 1995, 2000, *Meta-States: A New Domain of Logical Levels, Self-reflexiveness in Human States of Consciousness*, ET Publications, Grand Junction, CO.

Hall, Michael & Bodenhamer, Bob, 1997, *Figuring Out People: Design Engineering with Meta-programs*, Crown House Publishing, Carmarthen, Wales, UK.

Hearst, E., 1988, Fundamentals of Learning and Conditioning, in R. C. Atkinson, R. J. Hernstein, G. Lindzey, & R. D. Luce (eds.), *Stevens Handbook of Experimental Psychology*, Wiley, New York.

Hull, Clark, 1947, *Principles of Behavior*, Appleton, New York.

James, Tad & Woodsmall, Wyatt, 1988, *Time Line Therapy and the Basis of Personality*, Meta Publications, Cupertino, CA.

Jemmott, J. B. & McClelland, D. C., 1989, Secretory IgA as a Measure of Resistance to Infectious Disease: Comments on Stone, Cox, Valdimarsdottir and Neale, "Behavioral Medicine" (Summer, in Henry Dreher, 1995, *Immune Power Personality*, Penguin, New York.

Jung Carl, 1953, *On the Psychology of the Unconscious*, in H. Read, M. Fordham and G. Adler (eds.), *Collected Works of C. G. Jung*, Vol. 6, Princeton University Press, Princeton, NJ.

Kohlberg, L., 1969, Stage and Sequence: The Cognitive Developmental Approach to Socialization, in D. Goslin (ed.), *Handbook of Socialization Theory and Research*, Rand McNally, Chicago.

Kohlberg, L., 1971, From Is to Ought: How to Commit Naturalistic Fallacy and Get Away with it in the Study of Moral Development, in T. Mischel (ed.), *Cognitive Development and Epistomology*, Academic Press, York.

Korzybski, Alfred, 1933, 1994, *Science and Sanity: An Introduction to Non-Aristotelian Systems and General Semantics*, International Non-Aristotelian Library Publishing Company, Lakeville, CN.

Loevinger, Jane, 1976, *Ego-development: Conceptions and Theories*, Jossey-Bass, San Francisco, CA.

Mahler, Margaret, 1968, *On Human Symbiosis and the Vicissitudes of Individuation*, International University Press, New York.

Maslow, Abraham, 1962, *Toward a Psychology of Being*, Van Nostrand, Princeton, NJ.

Masterson, James, 1976, *Psychotherapy of the Borderline Adult: A Developmental Approach*, Bruner-Mazel, New York.

McClelland, D. & Kirschnit, C., 1988, The Effect of Motivational Arousal Through Films on Salivary Immunoglublin A, *Psychology and Health*, 2, pp. 31–52, in Dreher, H., 1995, *Immune Power Personality*, Penguin Books, New York.

McGaugh, J., 1983, Preserving the Presence of the Past: Hormonal Influences on Memory Storage, in Ernes Rossi, 1986, *The Psychobiology of Mind-Body Healing*, Norton, New York.

Miller, George, 1956, The Magical Number Seven, Plus or minus Two: Some Limits on Our Capacity to Process Information, *Psychological Review*, 63, 81-97.

Miramax Films, *The Englishman Who Went Up a Hill and Came Down a Mountain*, 1995.

Pavlov, Ivan, 1927, *Conditioned Reflexes*, Oxford University Press, London.

Perry, William, 1970, *Forms of Intellectual and Ethical Development in the College years*, Rinehart & Winston, New York, Holt.

Piaget, Jean, 1965, The Child's Conception of the World, in Dorothy Singer & Tracey Revensonm, 1996, *A Piaget Primer: How a Child Thinks*, Penguin, New York.

Rogers, Carl, 1961, *On Becoming a Person*, Haughton-Mifflin, Boston.

Rotter, Julian, 1954, *Social Learning and Clinical Psychology*, Prentice-Hall, Englewood Cliffs, NJ.

Satir, Virgini, 1983, *Conjoint Family Therapy*, Science and Behavior Books, Palo Alto.

Skinner, B. F., 1974, *About Behaviorism*, Random House, New York.

Swenson, Clifford, 1980, Ego Development and a General Model for Counseling and Psychotherapy, *Personnel and Guidance Journal*, 58, 5, 382–390.

Tillich, Paul, 1952, *The Courage to Be*, Yale Press, New Haven, CN.

Watzlawick, P., Weakland, J. & Fisch, R., 1974, *Change*, Norton, New York.

Weiten, Wayne, 1989, *Psychology: Themes and Variations*, Brooks-Cole, Pacific Grove, CA.

USA & Canada *orders to:*

Crown House Publishing
P.O. Box 2223, Williston, VT 05495-2223, USA
Tel: 877-925-1213, Fax: 802-864-7626
www.crownhouse.co.uk

UK & Rest of World *orders to:*

The Anglo American Book Company Ltd.
Crown Buildings, Bancyfelin, Carmarthen, Wales SA33 5ND
Tel: +44 (0)1267 211880/211886, Fax: +44 (0)1267 211882
E-mail: books@anglo-american.co.uk
www.anglo-american.co.uk

Australasia *orders to:*

Footprint Books Pty Ltd.
Unit 4/92A Mona Vale Road,
Mona Vale NSW 2103, Australia
Tel: +61 (0) 2 9997 3973, Fax: +61 (0) 2 9997 3185
E-mail: info@footprint.com.au
www.footprint.com.au

Singapore & Malaysia *orders to:*

Publishers Marketing Services Pte Ltd.
10-C Jalan Ampas #07-01
Ho Seng Lee Flatted Warehouse, Singapore 329513
Tel: +65 256 5166, Fax: +65 253 0008
E-mail: info@pms.com.sg
www.pms.com.sg

South Africa *orders to:*

Everybodys Books
Box 201321 Durban North 401, South Africa
Tel: +27 (0) 31 569 2229, Fax: +27 (0) 569 2234
E-mail: ebbooks@iafrica.com